Looking Backward at Us

Looking Backward at Us

William Raspberry

"DISCARD"

UNIVERSITY PRESS OF MISSISSIPPI
Jackson & London

Library of Congress Cataloging-in-Publication Data

Raspberry, William.
    Looking backward at us / William Raspberry.
        p. cm.
    ISBN 0-87805-535-5
    1. Afro-Americans—Social conditions—1975–   2. United States—
Race relations.   3. United States—Social conditions—1980–
I. Title.
E185.86.R36   1991   91-21565
                                                                      CIP

British Library Cataloging-in-Publication data available

Contents

Introduction

"Where do you get your ideas?"

It may be the question most frequently asked of newspaper columnists. My colleague Richard Cohen is given to answering, "There's a little shop on 14th Street..." I am inclined to respond: "Everywhere." But neither his whimsy nor my candor satisfies, and I think it's because the people who ask the question want to know something else: not so much the origin of the ideas but the source of the attitudes, the assumptions, the point of view that make each columnist's voice unique.

Looking back, I am persuaded that my own point of view— my philosophy, to call it by too grand a name—comes from my parents, James and Willie Raspberry of Okolona, Mississippi. It is influenced, of course, by the accidents of time and circumstance: being born into a family of educators, growing up black in the racially segregated Mississippi of the 1940s and 1950s, coming of age during the civil rights and women's rights revolutions, having the luck to have escaped the debilitating effects of poverty (primarily because everyone in our small town was poor), finding a profession that makes good use of my God-given abilities.

But mostly I owe whatever success I have managed to the lessons my parents taught. To begin with, they taught me to read. I don't mean simply that they taught me *how* to read. Virtually everyone in my first-grade class at Meridian Street High School learned how to read—probably because our teachers had not learned such impedimenta as "reading readiness." When I say I learned to read, I mean that my parents instilled in me a love of reading. They themselves read, and they derived such manifest pleasure from it that it seemed obvious to my siblings and me that reading must be fun. This, you must understand, was long before we came to the notion that beginning reading materials must be about things that are already familiar to students. It would have struck me as pointless, and unrelentingly boring, to read about things I already knew.

Reading was to become my passport to a world that was otherwise beyond my reach; my ticket to what E. D. Hirsch has called "cultural literacy."

At one level, Hirsch's notion that there is a finite number of things that literate Americans know, an identifiable list of things they have read, sounds like cultural imperialism of the worst sort; an assumption that certain books and ideas are better than others, not because of their intrinsic worth but because members of the cultural aristocracy have read them.

But my parents gave me to understand that true literacy is culture specific, and that there is value in becoming literate in the general American culture. Is that culture too white? Undoubtedly. Too European? No question of it. Efforts to broaden the definition of cultural literacy have my support and applause. But literacy in America also involves familiarity with the things that well-educated Americans know.

I won't defend Hirsch's list. He got caught in his own trap, that if the things that literate people know constitute a finite list, that list ought to be capable of reduction to writing. But if there are things that intelligent people know—whether those things show up in their response to "Wheel of Fortune" and "Jeopardy," or whether they manifest themselves in ordinary conversation or formal discourse—you have done yourself no favor to avoid learning these things. It is well to learn other things, of course: things with special relevance for your own history and circumstances. But if one is to be thought intelligent— if one is to *be* intelligent—it is vital to learn those things that have become a part of the American culture.

My parents chose that direction for themselves and for their children. They read for new knowledge, for understanding, for the sheer pleasure of it. And so did we.

It was my unquestioned belief that books were full of information and excitement and pleasure that kept me reading, that expanded my curiosity and (though I didn't know it at the time) got me ready for writing.

Yes, I learned grammar. But, looking back, I am convinced that the value I got from grammar had to do with correct word usage, varieties of expression and nice-sounding ways of saying things. I learned to diagram sentences because I had to. But I never saw the slightest use for it; I still don't. I also, beginning in junior high, learned to outline short themes, though, again, I never saw any utility in it. The truth is, I usually wrote my piece first and then proceeded to make an outline, not for me but for the teacher.

And I learned the nuts and bolts of grammar: in grade school and in high school. By the time I took freshman English at Indiana Central, where the emphasis was on grammar, it was a piece of cake. I could spot a gerund or a participle from across the street. I had, by then, mastered the logic of grammar. I understood why dangling participles were wrong; why misplaced appositional elements could lead to ambiguity; why it was important to take care to close quotations and parentheses. I never really learned why splitting infinitives should be an actionable offense, but I did learn to not split them.

My English Comp teachers, if any survive, would tell you that I also learned to write during my college years. They would be wrong. What I learned was some tricks: dropping short, punchy sentences in the middle of a series of long ones; putting important ideas at the beginning of sentences or else at the end (never in the middle); the use of irony.

But I didn't learn to write. Why? Because I had nothing to say, and no one to say it to. I was writing for an audience of one: a professor who had to read what I had written.

I'll tell you when I learned to write: when I took a job at

the *Indianapolis Recorder*, the summer between my junior and senior years at the University of Indianapolis. For the first time, I had information that I considered important and an audience that I thought needed the information. For the first time, I became aware of how easy it is for a reader to pass up my writing, or to stop reading after a few paragraphs. And that is when I learned to write leads that would capture a reader's attention and to use my little tricks to hold his interest. I learned to give statistics human form, to explain why things were important, to give a fair hearing to all sides of a controversy by taking pains to understand how someone could embrace a point of view other than my own.

After four years at the *Recorder* and (following two years in the Army) a year at the *Washington Post, I was writing reasonably well.* But I had the idea that I could write better if I spent time dissecting other people's writing. So I asked for permission to spend six months as a copy editor, where my job was to read other reporters' writing for clarity, content, factual and grammatical accuracy, taste, consistency of style—all those things that English teachers stress but which their students never seem to grasp.

It worked. I learned that being alert to holes—unanswered questions—in other people's stories helped me to avoid leaving holes in my own. I learned the value of off-beat approaches and humor, and I also learned to try out my off-beat ideas on other people before submitting them to my editors. I learned that long, complicated sentences were best broken up into simpler ideas.

And I learned one more thing: I learned to *hear* my words. That's something my teachers had neglected to teach me. I learned it by reading other people's copy. I learned to look out for the awkward phrases, the oddly juxtaposed sounds that cause a reader to stumble.

But that has to do with the *mechanics* of writing. Looking back, I see my parents' hands in the *content* of my writing. It was from my mother, the English teacher and amateur poet, that I learned to care about the rhythm and grace of words; it was from my father, the shop teacher, that I learned that neither end tables nor arguments are worthwhile unless they stand solidly on all four legs.

My parents taught me to think. They made me know it was all right to have a different view of things, to reach the unorthodox conclusion, to follow uncomfortable thoughts to their logical conclusions.

And they instilled in me the attitudes that mark the best of my work today. What are these attitudes? That virtually everyone can, given opportunity and motivation, achieve some measure of success; that most Americans want to do the right thing; that racial groups are more alike than they are different (or at any rate that the differences are more likely to be factors of economic and social conditions than of race *per se*); that people are likely to act on the basis of reliable information in their own self interest.

These attitudes are, like my colleague's "little shop on 14th Street," where I get my ideas. Thus, a recurring theme in my columns is the primacy of motivation and opportunity in helping minority children to break out of the conditions that entrap them. If readers are sometimes unsure as to where I fit on the left-to-right spectrum, it may be because I am more like liberals in my insistence on government-guaranteed opportunity, closer to conservatives in my belief that government can do very little to motivate people to take advantage of opportunity. Motivation must come from nearer home: from parents first and foremost, and failing that, from teachers and others with a personal interest in the children's success.

I resist the conservative notion that opportunity is more or less there for the taking in our free-market society, now that the racial barriers have been (officially) removed; opportunity is not real unless people are taught to see it and believe it. But I also resist the liberal impulse to feel sorry for people whose life chances have been artificially thwarted by the circumstances into which they were born. Pity encourages people to see themselves as powerless victims; sympathy—the ability to put oneself in the place of another—can point the way toward joint problem solving. Pity says: You poor dear! See what they've done to you! Sympathy says: Let's figure out what I can do to help you help yourself.

I once wrote that the unofficial theme song of Black America is "Nobody Knows the Trouble I've Seen." The reference was to the tendency to define ourselves by our suffering, in slavery and beyond; to communicate the idea that no one who is not black can understand us sympathize with our plight. It's a mistake. Just as you don't have to be Jewish to understand the imprint of the Holocaust on the Jewish psyche, you don't have to be black to understand what slavery and racial segregation have meant to African Americans. Anyone who genuinely tries can understand the debilitating effect of living one's life on the outside looking in—at least to the point of understanding why race is such an important part of our social and political calculations.

The things that unite us in our humanity are both more numerous and more important than the things that divide us by race and ethnicity. That is why I try to write about matters of race in terms that can have meaning for those who have not directly experienced race-based deprivation.

Indeed, while it is true that America's struggle for racial equality is made unnecessarily difficult by white inattention to the special history of blacks in this country, it may also be impeded by black overemphasis of race. Race, as a reader of my column suggested some years back, has become our all-purpose myth—and a destructive one at that. Mary Pringle, a Virginia educator said it occurred to her that Americans generally have lost the myths that give meaning to their lives, and that black Americans in particular suffer from the loss. The predominant surviving myth of black Americans, she said, is that of racism as the dominant influence in their lives.

Myths, she was careful to point out, are not necessarily false. Indeed, whether positive or negative, they are almost always based on actual group experience. But the nature of the operative group myth can make a profound difference in group outcomes.

"Racism is a reality, but it has been overcome by many and given way to opportunity and success." Those who have overcome it, she argued, have been moved by different myths: myths that paint them as destined for success rather than doomed to failure, myths that lead them to see themselves as members of a special group capable of overcoming all odds. That is the kind of myth that blacks need to cultivate, she said.

"Racism, though it is a reality, has been a destructive myth, giving greater power to the odds against success than exist in reality, making it harder even to *try*. What we need is a stronger, more powerful myth that is constructive and evokes a sense of identity and energy to move ahead."

Objective reality is the arena in which we all must perform. But the success or failure of our performance is profoundly influenced by the attitudes—the myths—we bring to that reality.

Two things flow from the racism-is-all myth that we have used to account for our difficulties. The first is that it puts the solution to our difficulties outside our control. If all our problems are caused by racism, and their solution dependent on ending racism, our fate is in the hands of people who, by definition, don't love us.

The second outcome of the myth is our inclination to think of our problems in terms of a failure of racial justice. Any discrepancy becomes, by that thinking, a claim against society. Income gaps, education gaps, test-score gaps, infant-mortality gaps, life-expectancy gaps, employment gaps, business-participation gaps—all now are talked about as if they had nothing to do with behavior and everything to do with race-based deprivation.

The problems indicated by all these gaps are real. But the belief that racism is their sole cause steers us away from possible solutions. It evokes a sort of central justice bank, managed by the government, whose charge is to ladle out equal portions of everything to everybody. It prompts us to think about our problems in terms of inadequate or unfair distribution. It encourages the fallacy that to attack racism as the source of our problems is the same as attacking our problems. As a result, we expend precious resources—time, energy, imagination, political capital—searching (always successfully) for evidence of racism, while our problems grow worse.

Is there another, more fruitful, approach for dealing with the racism that remains a fact of American life? I believe there is, and that it lies in learning to embrace a different myth—a myth that says: I am in control of my fate, and no one can stop me from undertaking the effort that is necessary to achieve the things I want. Of course racism will sometimes deny us the fruits of our exertion, and it must be fought. But this new myth's insistence that what we do is a more important determinant of our success or failure than what is done to us would save us from our single-minded focus on racism.

Some will insist, no doubt, that as long as racism exists, we simply have to focus on it; that to do otherwise is ostrich-like and simple-minded.

To them I say: All right, let us stipulate that racism is the overriding reason for our situation, and that an all-out attack on racism is our most pressing priority. Now let us suppose that we eventually win the fight against racism and put ourselves in the position now occupied by poor whites. What would you urge that we do next?

Pool our resources? Establish and support black businesses? Insist that our children take advantage of the opportunities that a society free of racism would offer? What should be our next steps?

Well, just for the hell of it, why don't we pretend that the racist dragon has been slain already—and take those next steps right now?

Do that, and we just might be surprised at the proud and hopeful picture we see some day when we are looking back at us.

On Education

IN SEARCH OF BETTER TEACHERS

LET ME ACKNOWLEDGE straight off that there are some outstanding actual and prospective public school teachers, including many who could, if they chose, pursue other, better-paid careers.

I hear about them from satisfied parents. I meet them in classrooms (including my own children's classrooms) and in teachers' colleges as I travel across the country.

Still, it is obvious—and documentable—that the academic competence of people who choose teaching as a career is on the decline. And it seems reasonable to suppose that that is a major reason for last week's disconcerting (though hardly surprising) report by the National Commission on Excellence in Education: that a "rising tide of [academic] mediocrity threatens our very future as a nation."

The academic ability of present and future teachers is, of course, not the only reason for that rising tide. The widespread abandonment of rigorous standards for students contributes to the threat. So does the deterioration in classroom discipline, parental involvement and respect for teachers.

But we can hardly expect public education to improve even to the levels of a generation ago, let alone reach the new heights demanded by an increasingly technological society, if the quality of entering teachers continues to decline.

It would be interesting to plot the decline in public school academic achievement alongside the increase in job opportunities for women. My guess is that there is a significant correlation. There was a time when the brightest of women became teachers because they could not hope to become doctors, engineers, lawyers, technicians and government or business executives.

That the brightest college women no longer look to careers as teachers is evident in the findings of the American College Testing Service. Of 19 major fields of study analyzed by the ACTS, education majors ranked 14th in English ability and 17th in math ability.

It may be that some of the brighter students would choose careers as teachers if teaching had the respect it once had. But the trend won't be reversed in any significant way until we start paying teachers at levels commensurate with what these brighter students could earn elsewhere.

Scott Thomson, executive director of the National Association of Secondary School Principals, makes just this point, noting that, three years ago, when Japan was just starting to put new emphasis on education, teachers were given a 25 percent salary increase. If Americans are serious about wanting to improve public education here, he said, "they must also be ready to make that kind of financial investment."

Thomson also stresses, as does the national commission's report, that the push to improve education cannot be limited to the schools. Parents must support tougher standards of performance and discipline; business must find ways to join in, both by lending technicians to teach part-time in the schools and by providing summer employment for teachers. And closer to home: "Many newspapers run the photos of every player on the all-metropolitan football team; how many papers run the photos of every honor student?"

But better pay for teachers may be the clearest statement of support for improving education and the quickest way of achieving it. The first beneficiaries of the higher salaries would of course be the present-day teachers, including the incompetents who have shaken our faith in public education. But that would be a price worth paying if the result were to get more of the very brightest college students into teaching, providing real options for school personnel officers who, as things are now, often are stuck with choosing the best of the duds.

(May 1983)

LET CHILDREN BE CHILDREN

THE JAPANESE HAD BEEN my last hope. I'd watched upscale parents turn their children into money-grubbers. I'd observed middle-class parents using their children as the means of competing with each other. I'd seen young-couple-on-the-make parents treat their children as obstacles to their own success. I'd seen downscale parents leave their children to their own devices, academically and morally.

But Japanese parents, I had thought, were managing pretty well. Oh, sure, they put a lot of pressure on their children to do well in school, but I took that to be a product of the way the Japanese educational system works. The impressive thing was how smart, how confident and how self-disciplined Japanese children seemed to turn out.

The Japanese have let me down. I've just read a *New York Times* report that Japanese parents, for all the advantage that their pro-family traditions and their ethnic homogeneity give them, are plagued by some of the same problems that beset their American counterparts—and for some of the same reasons, including pressure to succeed.

The news reports are startling to those of us who always thought of Japan as somehow special: Yokohama teen-agers assaulting a group of vagrants, killing three of them; a physically handicapped teacher stabbing a student after weeks of being abused and attacked by a group of boys; a 14-year-old girl beaten for three hours by a dozen of her classmates.

Most of the violent acts occurred during the anxiety-producing entrance exam period, which determines which young Japanese go on to top universities and which are condemned to working-class existences.

"Most parents," the mother of a third-grader told the *Times*, "are saturated with the idea that to go to a first-rank university leads to a job in a big company and that leads to a happy life."

But is it a happy life they want for their children? My guess is that a lot of these parents, like a growing number of American parents, would be thoroughly perplexed if they were offered a choice of happiness or success for their children (just as they would be perplexed if you offered them the choice of wealth or happiness for themselves). They might insist that the two things aren't separable, or that they needn't be mutually exclusive. But if they were forced to choose, I suspect a lot of them would opt for academic or economic success. Children who are happy but only marginally successful bring little prestige to their parents.

I don't mean to suggest that some parents want their children to be unhappy. The parents featured in that recent *Newsweek* magazine article, "Bringing Up Superbaby," surely wanted their children to be happy. But that isn't why they were pushing and shoving to get them into the "right" preschools, or buying them sawed-off violins, or shelling out money for the Better Baby Institute. They were doing these things, and buying books on baby math and pre-speech reading and computer programming for toddlers, because they want their children to be winners in a society they view as intensely competitive.

Ask these parents, or their Japanese counterparts, and they'll insist they want what is best for their children. But the way they go about it is more than a little frightening. A few of them might succeed in rearing geniuses. More of them are likely to wind up with driven, miserable adolescents. And some might be shocked to see that they have produced the senseless violence of the sort that is on the increase in Japan.

Obviously I'm not suggesting that parents shouldn't try to enhance the intellectual development of their offspring. But surely there must be something to be said for backing off and letting children be children.

(March 1983)

No. 1 in Math—
The Wrong Goal

BY THE YEAR 2000, our "education president" has promised, "U.S. students will be first in the world in mathematics and science achievement."

He also promised drug-free schools and 100 percent literacy and a few other impossible things before breakfast, but it was the math and science prediction that grabbed my attention.

Leave aside the fact the predictions were not commitments but only nebulous goals, devoid of any plan, money or program for achieving them. The question that comes to my mind is whether being "first in the world in mathematics and science" is a goal we ought to be taking seriously.

Of course it would please me to have the president's predictions come true. But how high on our list of priorities should it be to see that they do? How much of our meager educational resources (meager at least in terms of our willingness to tax ourselves to expand the resource pool) should we spend on the president's math and science goal?

It sounds heretical even to raise the question, so maybe I'd better explain myself. Yes, America needs more mathematicians and scientists if it hopes to remain economically competitive in the world. And, yes, we need our children to learn more of math and science than most of them are now learning.

But we also need to understand that those are two separable goals that may require quite different approaches.

We can produce outstanding mathematicians and scientists for American industry the same way we produce superlative athletes for the NBA and the NFL: by spotting talent early, developing it through intensive coaching and rewarding it with college scholarships and the prospect of huge salaries for those with "pro" potential.

But just as turning out professional-caliber athletes does not enhance the chances that a university will improve the physical education of most of its students, force-feeding those young-sters with an aptitude for math and science would do little for the math and science literacy of most students.

Improving the skills (athletic or scientific) of the wide range of students requires different techniques—and different coaches—than does the nurturing of a handful of superstars. We don't need all our children to become superstars in math and science. It may be heresy to ask, but what does it matter if the average Japanese or German kid knows more math and science than his American counterpart? If our top math and science students are as good as theirs, shouldn't that be enough?

Well, not quite enough. Too many American youngsters finish school with so little knowledge of math that they are incapable of qualifying for even entry-level jobs that require basic math skills. We need to do something about that.

But at the risk of offending (again) America's math teachers, what we need to do does not necessarily involve more higher-level math courses as a graduation requirement. It would be enough to make sure that all our children are, as the British say, numerate: that is, competent in the math and science they will need for work, for fun and for understanding their world.

That means they need a thoroughgoing understanding of

arithmetic and basic algebra. With these as a base, and access to whatever extra math they wish to take, they can learn the additional mathematics they may later require.

But while we are seeing to the basic numeracy of the great bulk of our children, we need also to develop the math and science potential of those children whose talents lie in that direction. And we also need to find out, as early in their academic careers as we can, which students have that special potential.

The thing I would caution against is the assumption, implicit in the president's pledge, that the way to increase our supply of scientists and mathematicians is to force *all* of our children into more science and math, to make the average American youngster competitive in math and science with the average Japanese kid.

The president's goal of making our children "first in the world" suggests that sort of post-Sputnik scramble that may have harmed as many children as it helped. Some children— the mathematically minded—no doubt delighted in and were benefited by the "new math" that took them inside number theory. But as math scores later revealed, a lot of our children were so confused by "new math" that they missed the chance to learn the math they needed.

Let's not ruin another generation of youngsters in the misguided goal of making them "first in the world" in math and science. I'd be happy if we could learn to turn out as a matter of routine literate, numerate young people capable of making it in the world.

(March 1990)

DO WE REALLY HAVE TO
STUDY COMPUTERS?

IN THE LATE-'60S MOVIE, *The Graduate*, an ostensibly money-wise party guest let Dustin Hoffman in on the big secret. His whispered one-word advice: "Plastics."

If the movie were being made today, the advice might be different: computers. Personal computers, as everybody knows, will shortly be an indispensable asset for any couple who fancy themselves reasonably intelligent, or who want their children to grow up with at least a chance of making it in the world. If we really care about our college-age children, we will urge them into computer-science majors, for that is where all the jobs will be.

Computer technology, we are told, will so alter the world that one will either become computer-wise or be cast on the economic scrapheap. And so we are buying personal computers. The proposal by Apple to donate a computer to every school in America set principals' mouths drooling across the land. We must see to it that the youngsters are computer literate, you know.

12

By 1986, every entering freshman at tiny St. Paul's College, in Lawrenceville, Va., will have his or her own personal computer.

Computers are the thing. And yet I wonder.

Most of the adults I know who own computers seem to use them primarily for word processing, which is like using the QE2 as a ferryboat. Their children, aside from that handful of budding geniuses who want to know what makes microchips work, use them principally for games.

Even the students at St. Paul's College will not need to know very much about computer technology. President S. Dallas Simmons has something much simpler in mind: "If the student is having a problem in a course, he can go to the library or the computer center and check out the appropriate software."

That's not what the savants who urge computers on us seem to have in mind. What they are telling us is that since computers are changing the world, we'd better get into computers if we expect to be employable.

It is, I suspect, bum advice. Of course the computer will change the way we do nearly everything we do. So did the automobile. And yet, it would have been a mistake if, 80 years ago, our grandparents had urged every school child to become an auto mechanic.

It's plain enough that computer technology, like every other technological breakthrough, will lead to the creation of jobs yet undreamed of. The mistake is in supposing that most of those jobs will be in computer technology. It is as impossible to predict just where the computer-spawned jobs will be as it would have been for a 1903 forecaster to look at Henry Ford's Detroit and predict the motel industry, automatic carwashes or suburban shopping centers.

Except for the math-and-engineering-minded, it's probably a mistake to push our youngsters too hard into computers. Seeing that they learn to use computers as instructional tools, for information retrieval, even for game-playing, makes good sense. But herding them sheep-like into computer technology does not.

The guess here is that as computers become more and more pervasive, more and more complicated, and more and more necessary, most of us will need to know less and less about them. And what we do need to know, the computer itself will teach us.

(October 1983)

EVERY KID NEEDS

SOME MANUAL ARTS

SUPPOSE MY EVENING'S TV-WATCHING was interrupted by the sound of an electric saw.

My first thought would be that some burglar was testing my power tools before making off with them; the second, that my 15-year-old son was about to do himself serious injury. (It would not enter my head that my daughters might be the source of the noise.)

That dismaying thought summarizes for me one of the things that I think has gone wrong with the way we do school. I was using my father's tools—handsaws, power saws, drill presses, miter boxes—long before I was the age my son is now. Neither my father nor I thought I would ever do woodwork for a living. Fooling around with tools was just something boys did.

More to the point, it was something the boys—at least at my small-town Mississippi school—were *taught* to do.

Today's youngsters, except for those deemed slow enough to

be consigned to shop class, are unlikely to be taught even how to make a shoeshine box or replace a frayed lamp cord. My prep school children are innocent of any such household skills and uninterested in acquiring them.

But it isn't just prep school children who are deprived of the chance to learn rudimentary manual skills. Probably most academically gifted youngsters are hustled into "academic" tracks whose focus is almost entirely on courses that will help them to get into college.

One result is that those who don't go on to college are likely to leave high school unable to earn a decent living.

It's a mistake, and not just for the boys.

A small part of the reason is cost. Shop classes large enough to accommodate all the children at a school take too much space and too much money. But a larger part is our either/or mentality with regard to academic and manual training. Smart kids do books; dumb kids do tools.

It is a dichotomy we would do well to abandon, for at least three reasons.

The first is that a lot of reasonably bright youngsters whose special gifts are in the manual arts are denied the chance to excel at what they do best. One result is that they lose interest in school and drop out.

The second, given the large number of young people whose formal education ends with high school, is that we are turning out high school graduates who have learned very little beyond reading, writing and basic math that will help them to land a decent job—as apprentice carpenters or masons or electricians, for instance.

The third is that even lawyers, engineers and professors ought to be able to make simple home repairs without calling in professional repairmen.

Lately, our attention has been focused on the Year 2000, by which time, we are told, a college degree will be the basic job credential. Even today, we are led to believe, college training is a virtual necessity for decently paid work.

Our schools are organized on that assumption. But, as

anybody who has had the bad luck to need a plumber or an electrician knows, it isn't true.

How might we do it differently? For one thing, every large public high school ought to have mandatory courses in such things as simple carpentry, sewing, typing, mechanics, electricity/electronics and upholstery, with students free to choose a course or two of special interest. Those who discover latent skills (or interest) as a result of these mandatory classes would have the option of "majoring" in them, while, at the same time, earning their college-entry credentials.

Thus, the student who leaves school after high school might easily find work as, say, an assistant to the manager of an apartment or small office building, with a clear path to a well-paid profession.

The student who goes on to college might earn some extra income by performing such things as word-processing or painting or repair.

And all students—drop-outs, high school graduates and PhD's alike—could save themselves a good piece of cash by knowing how to do some things for themselves.

Nor is it just the boys I have in mind. We are forever talking about the increase in the number of female-headed households, particularly among ethnic minorities. It is a problem, no doubt about it. But wouldn't these single mothers be a good deal better off if they knew how to free a sticking door, replace the ball on a toilet, change a faucet washer, build a bookcase or fix a lamp?

We are placing so much emphasis on college that we neglect to give our youngsters a chance at a noncollege career—by teaching them the things that all of us ought to know.

(July 1989)

GOOD MAJOR

The following remarks are excerpts from a commencement speech I gave recently at the University of Maryland:

APART FROM THE MINORITY OF YOU who will leave college for such trade schools as medicine or law or engineering, it is likely that by the time you are my age you will be doing something totally unrelated to your undergraduate major.

That does not mean that your undergraduate years will have been a waste; it only means that their value will consist primarily of the generalized information we call liberal arts. What your college education will have given you is someplace to stand while you figure out where to go.

It's all right. Take the word of someone whose major was, at various times, English, history, mathematics and pre-seminary, it's all right. You don't really need to know what you'll be doing 10, 15 or 20 years hence. And even if you wanted to know, you couldn't. Things are changing too fast. Time doesn't always make ancient good uncouth, but it regularly renders ancient majors irrelevant.

We could hazard some guesses as to what the major sources of the new jobs may be: computer technology and gene-splicing, to name two. These two technological breakthroughs will change our lives—change the way we do nearly everything we do—as dramatically as electricity changed the lives of my grandparents. But that doesn't mean that my grandparents should have become electrical engineers.

The vast array of career possibilities introduced by electricity did not require knowledge of electricity. The careers that recombinant DNA and microchips will make possible will not necessarily require knowledge of those arcane fields.

The new possibilities are unknown and unknowable. You cannot get ready for them in any specific way. I only hope that you have, during your college years, learned the art of flexibility; that you have learned how to learn. Because that will be your most valuable asset in the years ahead: your willingness to stay loose and to recognize opportunity when it comes along, even if it bears no direct relationship to your college major.

One more thing before I turn you over to the real world: your generation may be the first one in a good while whose members cannot automatically expect to outstrip their parents in professional attainment, in career success and in affluence. Many of you are already living in the biggest house and perhaps enjoying the most affluent life style you will ever experience. And yet you are faced with more pressure to succeed than perhaps any generation before you.

That combination, I suspect, is one of the causes of the fear and frustration young people are experiencing these days and also, I suspect, the reason for the startlingly high suicide rate for bright, academically successful young people.

I think there is a preventive for that sort of tragedy, and I urge you to try it. And that is not to compete with your parents, or even with your own contemporaries, solely in terms of what we call life style. Compete, rather, in your contributions to the general good of society.

If you are as lucky as I hope you are, you will leave college not as mere intellectuals but as educated men and women: educated (in Charles Silberman's phrase) to "feel and to act as well as to think."

Your best shot at happiness, self-worth and personal satisfaction—the things that constitute real success—is not in earning as much as you can but in performing as well as you can something that you consider worthwhile. Whether that is healing the sick, giving hope to the hopeless, adding to the beauty of the world, or saving the world from nuclear holocaust, I cannot tell you.

Your own talents, inclinations and ideals are your best guide. Just make sure that it is something that enriches your mind and your soul, not just your bank account.

All who know you expect you to do well. On this landmark day in your young lives, I urge you—seriously implore you—also to do good.

(May 1984)

ASIAN AMERICANS—

TOO SUCCESSFUL?

Is the academic success of Asian Americans too much of a good thing? Are the country's top-tier universities looking for ways to reduce the Asian presence on their campuses?

The group who stopped by my office the other day have no doubt. Some of the top universities, they say, have resorted to what amounts to a quota on Asian-American students in an effort to maintain whites as the dominant presence. Worse, they insist, it is being done dishonestly: on the pretext that affirmative action is the culprit.

"When we first raised the issue back in 1984, the University of California at Berkeley suggested to us that the drop in Asian-American enrollment was attributable to their affirmative-action efforts for underrepresented minorities," said Henry Der, executive director of the San Francisco-based Chinese for Affirmative Action. "That is simply not true."

What is true, he said, is that the rule changes haven't benefited the so-called "protected minorities"—mainly African

Americans, Hispanics and American Indians. The principal beneficiaries have been whites.

Der, along with Don Nakanishi of the UCLA faculty, Melinda Yee of the Organization of Chinese Americans, and Paul Igasaki, Washington representative of the Japanese American Citizens League, had been meeting with legislators and civil rights advocates to stress that fairness to Asians does not necessitate an attack on affirmative action.

To see why, it is helpful to understand that most competitive universities have what amounts to two different admissions pools. The first comprises those considered on the basis of grades and test scores. The second embraces the "protected" groups—underrepresented ethnic and geographic minorities, re-entering women, the disabled, the poor, those with special talents and those admitted under "administrative review"—usually the sons and daughters of alumni or other influential citizens.

Since Asian Americans are generally not considered under-represented, they compete primarily in the first group—in other words, with whites.

Thus when Berkeley, which had been looking at combined verbal and math scores on the Scholastic Aptitude Test, considered (but never implemented) imposing a minimum score of 400 on the verbal portion of the test, the effect, if not the purpose, would have been to favor whites (who tend to do well on the verbal portion) over Asians (who tend to score higher in math).

"The interesting thing about that verbal score of 400," said Der, who emerged as the unofficial spokesman for the group, "is that in 1984 the average SAT verbal score for Asian test-takers was 398."

In any case, Asian-American applicants at such schools as Berkeley, Harvard, Yale, Brown and Princeton have a lower admission rate than whites, although, according to the visitors, the whites' academic qualifications are no better. In fact, Berkeley Chancellor Ira M. Heyman apologized last year for the "insensitivity" of his university's admissions process, which, he said, "indisputably had a disproportionate impact on Asians."

Der and the others insist only that Asians be treated fairly vis-à-vis whites. That emphatically does not mean that they oppose affirmative action for the "protected groups."

They were at special pains to dissociate their constituencies from the resolution introduced last October by Rep. Dana Rohrabacher (R-Calif.), which, while ostensibly designed to eliminate discrimination against Asian Americans, is widely viewed as an attack on affirmative action generally.

"We see it as an attempt to pit minorities against each other," said Yee.

"We support affirmative action," Igasaki told me. "We have benefited from it in the past, and while we don't really need it now in terms of undergraduate admissions, there are a lot of areas where Asians do suffer discrimination, and we want to have that tool available to us. It wouldn't make sense for us to say now that we've achieved some success in university admissions, let's pull the ladder up after us."

It's an excellent point, practically and politically. The problem, which neither the visitors nor the society at large has resolved, is how to meet the conflicting demands of diversity and elemental fairness. For certain, artificial ceilings on Asian admissions is no answer.

Nakanishi repeated the point he made in a recent article in *Change* magazine:

"It seems that Asian-American applicants are evaluated exclusively with the non-minority, regular admission pool and tend to be strong candidates . . . However, because Asian-American applicants are counted as minorities, university officials also can boast about the racial diversity of their entering class.

"There is something at least peculiar, and perhaps insidious, about this relationship that demands closer and more serious attention."

(February 1990)

How Do You Justify

Separate Schools?

I DON'T HAVE A LOT OF TROUBLE deciding what I feel about single-sex (or single-race) schools. My difficulty is in trying to mold my inconsistent opinions into a principle.

For instance, I am utterly untroubled by the existence of a Mills College as a school for women. I understand how difficult it is for the most ambitious of women to rise to positions of leadership in male-dominated environments, and I also know the negative pressures even on pre-college girls, who often find that they must make a choice between popularity and leadership.

But if female-only schools are all right, what can be wrong with male-only schools? At the public high school level and lower, nothing much. Catholic educators have long believed that both boys and girls perform better in single-sex schools. It is at the college level that the misgivings—and the inconsistencies—arise. Why do we find it easier to sympathize with Mills College students who want their school to remain the way it has been for 138 years than with students at Virginia Military Institute, which has had a men-only policy for 152 years?

One answer is that Mills is private, while VMI is a state-supported institution. The public/private distinction is relevant because governments, unlike private organizations, have an obligation to provide equal opportunities for all citizens. But it doesn't change what I take to be the widely held view: all-female colleges are okay; all-male colleges smack of anti-female discrimination. What principle supports such a distinction?

The same difficulty applies to historically black colleges and universities. More and more middle-class black parents (including this one) are sending their children to black colleges. We believe our children may be better off socially and academically in an environment where race is not an issue. The evidence bears us out. But any proposal to establish and maintain colleges for the education of white students, no matter how comfortable an all-white environment might be for them, would strike us as patently racist. What is the principle that would justify one and not the other?

We can argue that historically black or women's colleges were created not out of a desire to discriminate but in reaction to discrimination against blacks and women. It is true, but so what? Isn't it better to eradicate the discrimination than to use it as the basis for further discrimination?

What is the principle that, in my mind, makes it all right to have nearly a hundred colleges for women, a Spelman or a Benedict College for black women, a Morehouse College for black men, and a few dozen co-ed colleges for black students but not quite all right to have predominantly white all-male colleges? Such a principle might include the following considerations:

■ *Fairness.* Gender- or race-specific schools are defensible for groups that have not yet made it to the American mainstream, but not for white men, who already dominate in the society.

■ *Diversity.* The idea of diversity should impel us toward inclusiveness, but it might also justify the maintenance of a diversity of choices, including gender- or race-dominant schools, as long as the goal is to increase the options for all.

■ *Nondiscrimination*. It is all right to have a school that is predominantly—even overwhelmingly—black, white, male or female, as long as it is not exclusively so. I'd be opposed to a rule that said whites may not attend Hampton or Howard, or that men may not attend Mills or Mississippi University for Women. As a matter of fact, many of the historically black colleges have white students, and many women's colleges have male students. The trouble with VMI is not that it is predominantly male but that it excludes females.

But all this still leaves me unable to articulate a principle I'd be prepared to defend. Would I support a single-sex option for public schools? Perhaps. As a matter of fact I have argued for boys-only classes, taught by male teachers, for inner-city public schools. Would I, by the same token, support a single-race option for public schools? Of course not—even if it could be shown that segregated schools enhanced the leadership prospects for black students and faculty. That would be nothing short of the discredited separate-but-equal notion the Supreme Court struck down a generation ago.

It's easy enough to know what seems right. Stating it as a principle is another matter.

(May 1990)

CHOICE IN EDUCATION

YOU'RE GOING TO BE HEARING more and more about "choice" in education during the next months and years—and not just from the political conservatives who have been pushing vouchers and tuition tax credits for the past decade and longer.

The new choice advocates, whose voices are changing the climate of the education debate, are not the conservative ideologues but ordinary men and women—often black and poor—who have given up on an educational system they are convinced has given up on their children.

They are people like Polly Williams, the Wisconsin state legislator, who has pushed through a voucher plan under which, starting this fall, 1,000 Milwaukee youngsters can attend any private nonsectarian school of their choosing, with the state paying up to $2,500 in tuition costs; or Lawrence Patrick, the Detroit school board president, who is pushing a plan that will combine Milwaukee-like choice with Chicago-like community control of public-schools.

Williams and Patrick are black, and it matters. As long as white conservatives were the driving force behind vouchers, tax credits and other choice mechanisms, the mostly liberal education establishment found it easy to discredit them as not really interested in the education of poor children but only in their own arcane doctrines.

No such charge can stick against Polly Williams, an inner-city single mother who twice headed Jesse Jackson's presidential campaign in Wisconsin. Her interest, she insists, is not in undermining public schools but in educating poor black children. They aren't being educated now, she says, because the school hierarchy has been more interested in perpetuating its own power and in promoting racial integration.

Like Patrick, her goal is not to empty the public schools but to force them to improve.

Choice, of course, embraces far more than tuition payments and community control. Indeed, it may be misleading to subsume under the single heading of "choice" the myriad plans that are either being developed or are already in place in an effort to make the public schools better.

In Chicago, choice means neighborhood school boards, complete with the power to hire and fire teachers and principals, as a means of freeing local schools from the stultifying distance and detachment of "downtown." In Minnesota, it means giving parents the right to send their children to any public school—even across district lines. In New York, it means freeing parents to design their own education programs. In East Harlem, for instance, huge schools have been transformed into a series of smaller ones which, while housed in a common building, employ their own distinctive approaches to organization and teaching.

The fascinating thing about all these schemes is how little they are involved with race. For a full generation following the 1954 Supreme Court desegregation decision, the civil rights establishment has focused on racial integration. The theory has been that the best way of giving black children an equal education is to get them into the same schools and classrooms as white children.

It has worked reasonably well in smaller school districts, where, for instance, two segregated and underfunded high schools could be merged into one. It has not worked well in the larger cities, where racial housing patterns have made integration achievable only by wide-scale busing and, more recently, magnet schools designed to attract white students.

It is true that the magnet schools have generally been both superior and integrated. But it is also true that the educational needs of the majority of black children have been sacrificed to the efforts to attract white children.

As Williams put it, for example, Milwaukee's desegregation plan principally benefited whites drawn to the magnet schools and black students who were either lucky enough to be included or whose parents were willing to "put their babies on the bus at 5:30 in the morning and not see them again until 6:30 in the evening."

She wants better opportunities for all children. But despite her success in the state legislature, her battle for choice is far from over. A suit against the plan, filed by a coalition including teachers, administrators and the president of the Milwaukee branch of the NAACP is now before the Wisconsin Supreme Court.

Interestingly, while it speaks of uniformity and standards and authority, the suit is virtually silent on the question of instructional quality. As Elizabeth Kristol, of the Ethics and Public Policy Center, noted in the *Post* [op-ed, June 22]:

"Not once in the petition are the relative merits of the Milwaukee public and private schools assessed in terms of the education or educational climate they offer children. There is no mention of courses of study, rates of graduation, reading scores, school safety, or the presence or absence of drug use. In short, the petition opposing the parental choice program does not touch a single issue that a parent of a school-age child cares about."

What Williams, Patrick and a growing band of choice activists care about is quality education for their children. And unless I misread the mood of millions of frustrated black parents, they are going to find an awful lot of support.

(July 1990)

BLACK KIDS NEED

STANDARD ENGLISH

IT'S EASY TO OVERSIMPLIFY these things, but I have an idea that the best thing that teachers could do for black students is to teach them, starting as early as possible, to speak English well.

Yes, standard English. The sort of English, written and spoken, that we automatically associate with intelligence.

The counterarguments, easy enough to anticipate, are mostly wrong. It is true that standard English is just another dialect in a country full of them, no more consistent or inherently correct than any other dialect. No matter. Standard English—not Cajun or hillbilly or West Indian patois or Black English—is the language that marks an American man or woman as educated.

It is true, too, that inner-city black children aren't the only ones who have difficulty with the standard dialect. So do Hispanics, Asians, Europeans and others whose home language is not English. But black youngsters—particularly the boys—are virtually the only ones who actively resist learning standard English. The resistance costs them heavily, often for the rest of their lives.

I think I understand some of the reasons for the resistance. I remember wondering why so many of London's East Enders cling to their Cockney dialect, even while listening daily to the standard English spoken on the BBC and the "telly." It was clear to me that to be identified as a Cockney was to be thought lower class, poorly educated and not very bright. Why didn't they, at least when they ventured beyond the sound of the Bow Bells, abandon their home accent as an unnecessary millstone to their economic and social progress?

The answer, I soon learned, was fear. Suppose they gave up Cockney and, with it, their link to a special place and people, and still fell short of acceptance. They might find themselves in a sort of no-man's land, neither what they aspired to be nor yet what they were born.

Something very similar may be happening here. Children of the black slums, and not only the slums, resist the "enwhitenment" of standard English, fearing to cut themselves off from their roots while still not being accepted in the world where standard English is the norm.

It's worse than that. A black youngster who speaks "proper" English may find himself in endless playground squabbles, ridiculed and even physically assaulted, for acting "white." Ghettoese becomes the language of machismo.

I know boys who come from homes where standard English is routinely spoken who work at learning Ghettoese in order to win acceptance by their black peers. Girls somehow manage to escape the problem, and perhaps that is one reason why, around age 14 or 15, they tend to start being more careful with their speech.

Teachers, to return to my original point, could be of enormous help. A sympathetic but tough teacher might tell her young charges that it is of no concern to her what language they use on the playground. But in her classroom, the only acceptable dialect is standard English. She might explain that different circumstances dictate different usages: Black English on the playgrounds, archaic "thees" and "thous" in church, and standard English in the personnel office, on the job and in the classroom. If everybody had to speak the standard in the classroom, the stigma would disappear.

Youngsters thus would accomplish what educated black men routinely accomplish: a sort of bilingualism that renders them equally at home at work and at play.

Not only would they find themselves more employable upon leaving school, but they might also find their schoolwork a good deal easier. Since their texts are written in standard English, routine familiarity with the standard could save them the extra translation from written standard to spoken standard to the Black English of their ordinary speech.

And how could teachers help them to acquire standard English without eroding their innate pride in black culture?

One retired teacher of my acquaintance used to do it by explaining that so-called Black English is nothing more than the language slaves learned from their ignorant white overseers.

There are no doubt other ways of accomplishing the same end. However it's done, I can see nothing but good coming from helping young people—black youngsters in particular—acquire facility with the only language that confers instant respect.

(October 1986)

CODE-SWITCH BLACK
ENGLISH CAREFULLY

YOU WOULD NOT BE SURPRISED in the least to hear, say, your local judge use one style of speech as a participant in a neighborhood softball game, another when he's on the bench, and a third when he offers a prayer at church.

Linguists call it "code-switching," the ability to change from one language style to another, as circumstances dictate.

It's what most successful adults do without thinking about it, and it's what most of us—including the parents at Burnt Mills Elementary School—want our children to learn.

But Burnt Mills, in suburban Montgomery County, Md., is trying to accomplish a specific type of code-switching: to teach black children to shift easily between the "Black English" many of them speak and the more formal dialect of the classroom, the public forum and the personnel office. For some black parents, it's too specific for comfort.

Their objection is less to the idea of having their children learn standard English than to having them singled out on the basis of race for the voluntary program. The letter announcing the after-school program went only to parents of the school's black fifth graders.

The creators of the experimental project, a group of minority speech and language pathologists, believe it makes more sense to work with students who speak more or less the same informal language rather than include white or foreign-language speakers, who may have different problems.

But for some parents, the singling out suggests racial insensitivity.

"Clearly I think all youngsters in this society need to be taught the standard language," Hanley Norment, president of the Montgomery Chapter of the NAACP, said. "Otherwise, they cannot be meaningfully employed as they grow up. But the assumption (at Burnt Mills) was that all black kids obviously have a problem with the language and that their parents undoubtedly do, too, so we'll just use a broad-brush approach rather than sensitively looking at the needs of each child."

It's a good point, and other schools participating in the county-wide experiment have used different methods of recruiting participants.

One principal, for instance, sent letters to parents of 11 children he thought could benefit from the program.

Recruiting methods aside, the Montgomery County program makes a good deal of sense, both in its conception and in its approach.

"Many black students come to school speaking a language that is an important part of their rich Afro-American culture, commonly referred to as 'Black English,'" said the letter sent out to the Burnt Mills parents.

"However, the school and work setting use a language that is more formal—referred to as 'Standard English.' The challenge is for our students to learn to move between 'Black English' and 'Standard English' and speak them both successfully, thereby increasing their school and career opportunities."

The program uses drama, music, art, storytellers and tape recordings to drive home the appropriateness of different speech styles for different occasions. It carefully avoids suggesting to the children that they need to rid themselves of their informal speech patterns, focusing instead on the need to acquire the more formal style as well.

There's no doubt in my mind that the program, if successful, could make a profound difference, not just in future employment but also in present-day academic achievement. I suspect that much of the "culture bias" of standardized tests is in fact language based.

Children uneasy with the language of testing may find it difficult to answer questions correctly even when they know the material. Reading is more difficult when the material to be read is in an unfamiliar language style, and difficulty in reading may lie behind sub-par performance in everything from English to mathematics.

Nor do I doubt that children who are fluent in standard English feel smarter and, as a result, learn more easily.

The question is whether there is anything race specific about these general notions, or whether, as some black parents have argued, code-switching skills should be taught to all children.

My view is that both notions are correct. There's no question that too many children of all races are leaving school with less than adequate competence in reasoning, problem-solving and communication—all language related.

Nor is there any doubt that a part of the problem is race-specific—that the limitations of "Black English" cross the bounds of geography and social class.

What might make sense is for children to be given the opportunity to begin their specialized language instruction in classes with their racial peers, then be moved on to more generalized instruction in the standard dialect.

However it's done, though, the important thing is to give the youngsters an important skill, not to convey the academically crippling notion that there's something wrong with them.

(February 1991)

ROLE MODELS AND THE

EDUCATION OF BLACK BOYS

THE NUMBERS ARE DISMAYING, baffling and unsurprising. Black males in suburban Prince George's County public schools are in trouble: academic and social.

They are twice as likely to be enrolled in "special education" English classes as in English classes for the talented and gifted; less likely to be enrolled in college-prep courses (only 44 black males in the entire county are taking calculus); far more likely than other students to be suspended or expelled, and though they represent only a third of the district's enrollment, they make up nearly half of the students receiving special-education services.

Nor is the situation in Prince George's unusual. The same thing is happening to black males right across the country. The difference is that Prince George's is trying to do something about it.

An advisory committee appointed by the school superintendent has looked at the problem and come up with a number of recommendations for change. That's the good news. The bad news is that much of what the group has recommended is (in my view) irrelevant, immaterial or impossible.

For instance, it cites statistics that place the county's schools near the bottom of the state in per-pupil expenditures for textbooks, library resources and instructional materials. Obviously it makes sense to improve these resources if in fact they are inadequate.

But their presumed inadequacy does not explain why black boys should fare less well academically than whites, Asian Americans—or even black girls.

A review of textbook and library lists found "only a superficial rendering of the perspectives and experiences of African Americans, women and other cultural groups." But while any reasonable person can see the value of cultural, literary and historical inclusion, I doubt that substituting Chinua Achebe, James Baldwin or Mary Frances Berry for William Shakespeare, Nathaniel Hawthorne or the white authors of high school history texts would significantly raise the relative academic performance of black boys.

Only 6 percent of classroom teachers in the county are black men. I devoutly wish there were more—in Prince George's and elsewhere. But they don't exist, either in the ranks of certified teachers or in the freshman classes of the nation's teacher-training institutions.

Some of the proposals of the advisory committee are eminently achievable but will require the cooperation of parents and the wider community: expanded mentoring and counseling programs, more emphasis on self-esteem and increased rewards for academic achievement. Even so, there is reason to wonder if these improvements would bring the performance of black boys up to the level of black girls.

Young black men represent a special problem in America (and not just in the schools), and it may be worthwhile to look for factors that place them at special disadvantage. For example, it may be that black boys strike their teachers (including middle-class black teachers) as alien, hostile and even menacing. If this is so—and if teachers, on the basis of sad experience, also expect less from black boys—it shouldn't surprise us that black boys achieve less.

It seems clear (look at the unemployment statistics) that black males whose education ends with high school graduation do less well than their female counterparts in the job market. If the boys see their job prospects as slim, is there any wonder that they see less utility in classroom performance?

There are other problems that, for a variety of reasons, put black boys in a special, and specially worrisome, category. But the most obvious one is hardly dealt with in the advisory committee's report: Black boys are more likely than any other group to grow up in families that do not include a parent of their own gender.

White and Asian youngsters are more likely than blacks to spend their formative years in two-parent households. And even in single-parent homes, black girls usually have their mothers to teach them how responsible women are expected to behave.

Black males may be peculiarly susceptible to learning the lessons of manhood not from their homes but from the streets. This, I suspect, is one of the key reasons why they confuse manliness with machismo, why they equate manhood with the ability to "take care of themselves" in physical, rather than intellectual, contests, and why so many of them scorn academic exertion as either effeminate or "acting white."

Clearly we need to undertake efforts to counter these crippling notions: both by preaching as loudly as we can the importance to the proper development of children of having both parents around and by finding ways to teach the correct lessons of manhood to children from fatherless homes.

I think we can do it. But first it is necessary to recognize the problem. My own sense is that the dearth of positive male role models has more to do with the academic underachievement of black boys than inadequate expenditures, Eurocentric textbooks or a shortage of male teachers.

(August 1990)

LEARNING AND LOST CULTURE

IF YOU HAVE THE FEELING that you're the only one who doesn't understand the philosophical flap over "culture" and education in America, move over. There are two of us.

I have heard the contention that the reason American education serves black and Hispanic youngsters so poorly is that school is hopelessly Eurocentric. The need is either for multiculturalism (if the prescriber is politically moderate and integrationist) or Afrocentricism (the view of the self-consciously black and radical).

I have seen scholarly tracts claiming that minority children can't learn because their textbooks, their schools—the entire culture—ignore their Hispanic or African heritage, making it impossible for them to develop the self-esteem necessary for learning. I have read the academics who insist that the problem is that schools take too little account of African (or Hispanic) learning styles.

And I confess I don't understand any of it.

Mind you, I am not talking about such efforts as Carter G. Woodson's "Negro History Week" (or its present incarnation as Black History Month) calculated to make up for the exclusion from official texts of the contributions of nonwhites and to bring home to black children that their color (and the American bias against it) is no insuperable bar to achievement. I understand that well enough.

I understand, too, a child is unlikely to do well in school if he believes his teacher doubts his ability to learn, or is contemptuous of his group, and I understand that the attitudes some children learn at home (for instance that school is lower priority than, say, contributing to the family finances) militate against academic success.

What I don't understand is the notion that the reason these youngsters suffer is that their Africa- or Central-America-based "culture" is being denigrated in favor of Eurocentric imperatives and that the cure lies in resurrecting their lost culture.

Take the question of "learning styles." Is there some peculiarly African approach to assimilating information that puts black children at a disadvantage in American schools? Janice Hale-Benson of Cleveland State University posits an African style of learning that is "relational"—that features approximation, contextual meaning and a focus on people, in contrast to a European style that is analytic, emphasizes precision and focuses on things.

I don't doubt that the two styles exist, but I'd guess they are about as likely to explain boy-girl differences—or social class differences—as black-white ones. In any case, a good teacher will try different approaches to put a lesson across.

Diane Buck Briscoe, who with Catherine Gurba has produced a resource book for adult-education teachers in Florida, take the practical approach that teachers should learn to interpret and understand the divergent behavior of students without negatively stereotyping them. Thus, if some youngsters learn better in groups than as individualistic competitors, the teacher ought to consider experimenting with cooperative learning. If some students respond more to family values, then efforts might be made to involve parents.

This makes sense, no matter the color of the children or their teachers. No sensitive or intelligent teacher will denigrate what a child already knows—whether that prior knowledge involves comparison shopping, an ear for harmony and rhythm or the ability to cope with life on the mean streets of the inner city. Smart teachers not only understand the necessity of building on what a child has already learned but also learn to identify the impediments to learning that may be a part of the child's home environment.

For instance, Briscoe and Gurba note that a teacher raised to believe in the overriding importance of education may question the commitment of a Puerto Rican student who is frequently absent from class. "However, education is subordinate to family duties in the culture of Puerto Ricans, and the learner may not be behaving in a culturally irresponsible manner by missing school to attend to family obligations. Indeed the learner may even forsake education entirely and drop out of school in order to work and supplement family income."

If that is just another way of saying different children come to school with different attitudes and expectations, I can understand it.

What I don't understand is the contention that the differences are ethnically based: that there is some peculiarly European or African or Asian way of processing information, and schools have an obligation to reacquaint students with their cultural styles.

(September 1990)

EURO, AFRO AND OTHER
ECCENTRIC "CENTRICS"

THERE ARE AT LEAST TWO WAYS of looking at culture and education in this country. One is to look at the cultural rivulets and tributaries that produce the ever-changing amalgam we recognize as American culture. The other is to focus on, celebrate and work at isolating the different streams.

The first finds expression in the idea of multiculturalism, the second in efforts to lift one culture above the rest, either as intrinsically superior or as peculiarly accessible to the ethnic descendants of that culture.

The first is as old—and as imperfectly observed—as the notion of America as a pluralistic society. At its best, it celebrates the contributions of outstanding members of all ethnic groups while teaching children that genius is independent of ethnicity. The second, which seeks to inspire children of minority groups by teaching them that the *groups* from which they are descended are somehow special, seems little more than a mirror image of white superiority.

Diane Ravitch, writing in the *American Scholar* magazine, has come up with an interesting look at the two approaches.

"The pluralists," she says, "seek a richer common culture; the particularists insist that no common culture is possible or desirable. Advocates of particularism propose an ethnocentric curriculum to raise the self-esteem and academic achievement of children from racial and ethnic minority backgrounds. Without any evidence, they claim that children from minority backgrounds will do well in school *only* if they are immersed in a positive, prideful version of their ancestral culture...

"The pluralists say, in effect, 'American culture belongs to us, all of us; the U.S. is us, and we remake it in every generation.' But the particularists have no interest in extending or revising American culture; indeed, they deny that a common culture exists."

The particularist argument is heard most frequently these days by advocates of new teaching approaches for African-American children. Their contention is not merely that children of African descent have different "learning styles" from those of European or Asian background but that black children cannot be properly taught if the schools employ (as they do) a "Eurocentric" framework.

Molefi Kete Asante of Temple University puts it bluntly: "It is difficult," he says, "to create freely when you use someone else's motifs, styles, images and perspectives."

His proposal: African Americans should choose African names (he did), embrace African dress and religion and, taught by black teachers, learn to love their own culture.

"Do not be captured by a sense of universality given you by the Eurocentric viewpoint," he warns. "Such a viewpoint is contradictory to your own ultimate reality."

There are a couple of problems with this notion. The first is the questionable assumption that black children, with only the vaguest notions of their African ancestry, can be inculcated with African culture more easily than the American culture to which they are daily exposed. The second is that even if they could, would it not make them less competent in the culture in which they have to compete?

Ravitch, an adjunct professor of history and education at Teachers College, Columbia University, puts the questions this way:

"Is there any evidence that the teaching of 'culturally relevant' science and mathematics will draw Mexican-American children [presumably inspired by being told that the Mayans made modern mathematics possible by inventing the concept of zero] to the study of these subjects? Are children who learn in this way prepared to study the science and mathematics that are taught in American colleges and universities and that are needed for advanced study in these fields? Will Mexican-American children lose interest or self-esteem if they discover that their ancestors were Aztecs or Spaniards, rather than Mayans?"

That last question is particularly important in that it demonstrates some of the misuses of the term "culture." Anyone who knows anything about Africa, for instance, understands that there is no single "African" culture from which black Americans are descended. While some Africans were establishing a university at Timbuktu, others were engaged in slavery or tribal warfare or cannibalism. Some Africans were monotheists, while others were animists. As with their European counterparts, some were promoting brilliant philosophies while others were savages.

The point is not that American students (not just black students) should be led to ignore cultures other than that derived principally from Europe. The point is that individuals from every ethnic background have contributed to the American culture, and it seems silly that we should be asked to give it up as somehow alien.

The need is not to reach back for some culture we never knew but to lay full claim to the culture in which we live.

(September 1990)

AFROCENTRISM (CONTD.)

THE RESPONSE TO A PAIR of recent columns on Afrocentric education suggests at least three possibilities: 1. I did a poor job in stating my reservations. 2. The readers who disagree with me are misguided. 3. I was wrong.

On the chance that the first alternative is the correct one, let me try once more. First, I had hoped to make clear the distinction between two categories of proposals. One would include the history and cultural contributions of African Americans in our classroom accounts of American history and culture. The other would replace the emphasis on the European antecedents of the American culture with a new emphasis on African culture. The first, though too little practiced, is no longer controversial. I simply do not know people who dispute the notion that black Americans are too often the invisible men and women of American history; that they are too often discussed as problems in the nation's history rather than as contributors to it, and that this neglect demands correction.

It was the second view that concerned me. I expressed my doubt of the proposition, increasingly heard, that neglect of African culture in classrooms accounts for the academic difficulties of black American children. And it seemed obvious to me that whatever the value to black children of learning about ancient African cultures, their success in America requires that they learn to cope with the American culture.

But what of the role of ethnic pride in the self-esteem that is necessary for learning? The assumption of many advocates of Afrocentrism is that black children cannot think well of themselves unless they are taught they are descended from the builders of the pyramids, the developers of language and mathematics and tool technology, the founders of human civilization; that they cannot have pride in themselves unless they first have pride in their African origins.

I suspect the opposite is nearer the truth. If you don't believe you amount to much, you're not likely to have much interest in learning about your antecedents. A dispirited black child is as likely to be confirmed in his low self-opinion by much of what is going on in present-day Africa as to be uplifted by what happened in ancient Egypt. If, on the other hand, you think you're pretty wonderful, you may be interested in learning how such a wonderful person came to be.

As it turns out, nearly all the advocates of Afrocentrism will acknowledge that they had achieved a good measure of academic success before they discovered Africa; that it was curiosity triggered by their success that got them interested in learning about Africa rather than the other way around, and that the overwhelming source of the self-esteem that produced their academic success was their own families.

Even if I'm right about this, isn't it possible that immersion in the cultural contributions of Africa could help to engender pride in prideless black children? I grant the possibility, but it doesn't seem all that likely: no more likely, for example, than that black children discouraged by their own dismal circumstances will overcome that discouragement if they are taught about Nat Turner, Charles Drew or other heroes, scientists,

inventors or academics. They need to know about these contributors to the American culture—and so do white children.
But I doubt there is any academic magic in knowing about
them. And I think that at least a part of the push for Afrocentrism
is a search for academic magic: some button of ethnic pride,
some lever of unique learning style that can be activated to
transform discouraged and academically uninterested students
into scholars.

Of course, let all children learn about the contributions of
the great variety of cultures to the culture we call American; let
them also learn about the ancient cultures of their people, at
least so long as it does not substantially reduce the time
available for learning how to cope in present-day America.

But it seems to me black Americans who have achieved
some success in this country owe it to black children to tell
them how they did it. We need to talk to them about those
magic moments when we discovered white people had no lock
on intelligence, when—and by what means—we learned we
were bright and capable and what was necessary to translate
that potential into success. It may be that success can be
reached by a different route than worked for us, and Afrocentrism
may well be one possible route. But that's speculation. All we
can really know and share is what worked for us.

(October 1990)

On Criminal Justice

CRAZY? SO WHAT?

HERE WE GO AGAIN. Washington's alleged master burglar and accused murderer of Dr. Michael Halberstam, who supposedly caught him in the act, has asked, through his lawyer, for a hearing to determine his mental competency.

The man charged with the murder of John Lennon was in a Bellevue mental ward almost before the gun smoke had blown away.

The clear implication is that Bernard Welch and Mark David Chapman will plead innocent by reason of insanity when they come to trial for murder. With luck, one or both may even manage to avoid trial altogether.

The very possibility is one of the things that drive me batty about our criminal justice system. I'm willing to suppose that Welch and Chapman—if they in fact did what they are accused of doing—are crazy. Welch's lawyer suggests that "there might be some pattern of compulsive behavior which might have its roots in mental illness."

Perhaps. The multimillion-dollar stash police found in his elegant home clearly suggests that the alleged burglary spree wasn't the product of economic desperation.

Chapman, who allegedly bought a gun, quit his job in Hawaii and flew to New York for the express purpose of killing a man against whom he had no rational beef, may be, as a New York cop called him, a "nutcake."

But if a non-lawyer may legitimately entertain such questions: so what? Shouldn't it be the first order of business to answer the fundamental question: did they do it? And how can we do that unless they are brought to trial?

I'm jumping the gun, of course. There is no reason to suppose—yet—that they won't be tried. After all, the lawyer for David Berkowitz, accused in the "Son of Sam" killings, found a couple of psychiatrists willing to pronounce the suspect mentally incompetent and incapable of participating in his own defense. Berkowitz was tried and convicted anyway. Chapman already has been transferred from Bellevue to a jail cell.

But still, our unwillingness to separate the question of *whether* an accused committed the act he is charged with from the more problematical question of *why* he did it strikes me as wrongheaded. So does the notion that an otherwise criminal act is not a crime if it is the product of mental disorder.

You need look no further than last week's newspapers to see the mischief that can follow from this notion. I refer to the story, out of Chicago, that the man accused of beheading his girlfriend and mailing her toes to Gerald Ford and Alexei Kosygin has been recommended for release from the mental institution to which he was committed after the court found him innocent of murder by reason of insanity.

Psychiatrists say he is sane now, and, therefore, there is no further reason to keep him confined.

I'll grant that the acts of which he was accused were the product of a sick mind, if only because they were so singularly bizarre. But it wouldn't take much to convince me that nearly all of the most outrageous crimes are the products of sick minds. But again: so what? I'd be willing to let these crazies serve their statutory time in a mental lockup instead of the state pen, but that's about as far as I'd go.

My faith in psychiatry to cure these sickies is about on a par with my faith in the ability of prisons to rehabilitate the officially sane.

Sometimes the inmates of prisons and mental institutions get better; sometimes they don't. I count it a worthy thing to try to increase the number of inmates who do improve.

But why should that have any bearing on whether rapists and murderers and madmen serve out the time the law prescribes for their offenses? After all, we imprison people for what they have done, not for what they are, or what they fail to become.

(December 1980)

TAKE AWAY THE FIFTH

ROBERT M. KAUS HAS DELIVERED himself of an audacious, shocking, illiberal proposition: the Fifth Amendment of the U.S. Constitution ought to be abolished.

Ever since I saw his piece in the December issue of *Washington Monthly* (of which Kaus is an editor), I've been looking for flaws in his argument. I haven't found any.

His point is that the amendment was a mistake that protects only the guilty and does nothing for the innocent; that it is, in short, a constitutional absurdity.

And so it seems—if not in the plain words of the self-incrimination clause at least in the prevailing interpretation of what the clause means.

Presumably Kaus himself might not find the actual words objectionable: "No person . . . shall be compelled in any criminal case to be a witness against himself." If that means that law-enforcement officers have no right to compel a confession or to require a suspect to provide the authorities with any information that might be used against him, it seems reasonable enough.

But the court insists that it means more. It means that a law officer cannot even ask the questions, once the suspect invokes the amendment's protection.

Take this example: A man suspected of murdering a little girl is arrested in Davenport, Iowa. The police agree not to interrogate him until he has been transported 160 miles to Des Moines and given a chance to talk to his lawyer there.

During the trip, one of the escorting officers makes a speech: "They are predicting several inches of snow tonight, and I feel that you yourself are the only person that knows where this little girl's body is, and if you get a snow on top of it you yourself may be unable to find it. I feel that we could stop and locate the body, that the parents of this little girl should be entitled to a Christian burial for this little girl who was snatched away from them on Christmas Eve. I do not want you to answer me; I don't want to discuss it any further. Just think about it as we're driving down the road."

The suspect, Robert Williams, thought about it and finally told the officers where to turn off the main road. He took them to where the dead girl lay.

The Supreme Court overturned the subsequent conviction on the ground that the officer's speech constituted interrogation. And since Williams had not made a "knowing and intelligent waiver" of his right not to be interrogated, his subsequent confession should not have been admitted into evidence.

The casebooks are full of such rulings—including the famous *Miranda* ruling, requiring that the would-be interrogator warn the suspect of his right to remain silent and to have a lawyer present.

The court has extended the Fifth Amendment protections right into the courtroom, where it is now deemed unconstitutional for a prosecutor even to let the jury know that a defendant has declined to testify, lest that fact be taken as evidence that he has something to hide.

Kaus says it makes no sense.

What can possibly be wrong, he asks, with simply calling a suspect to the witness stand and asking him to testify? "If he admitted the crimes, he would be convicted. If he maintained his innocence and his story created a 'reasonable doubt' in the jury's mind, he would go free." And if he refused to answer, even on the witness stand, "the jury could take his silence for what it would in fact be—a powerful piece of evidence pointing to his guilt."

As Kaus makes clear, the issue is not torture or the so-called "third-degree." It is simply a matter of asking a defendant to tell his story—and of letting a jury draw reasonable inferences from his refusal to tell it.

Other parts of the Bill of Rights, Kaus contends, are designed to protect all citizens. "But 'the Fifth,' almost by definition, protects only the guilty."

He says it ought to be abolished.

(December 1980)

MAYBE SCHMOKE IS RIGHT

ABOUT DRUGS

BALTIMORE MAYOR KURT SCHMOKE, who startled a lot of us when he urged that we consider legalizing drugs, is starting to make more and more sense these days.

It isn't that Schmoke has marshaled new arguments since he first made his proposal a year ago. What gives new force to his position is the increasing practical difficulty of keeping the drugs illegal.

I'm not yet ready to concede that he is right. I still worry that legalization would tempt untold thousands of nonusers to try the stuff and that some among them would find themselves with hard-to-kick government-induced crack habits. I wouldn't want to add to the problem of drug addiction.

But what all of us have known in the back of our minds is becoming clearer with each passing day: that the harm done by our attempts to enforce antidrug laws is greater than the harm done by the drugs themselves.

The D.C. trial of alleged drug kingpin Rayful Edmond III

makes the point in ways that no theoretical construct ever could.

Not only did the court have enormous difficulty in empaneling a jury (the judge finally resorted to the unprecedented step of keeping the jury both sequestered and anonymous), but the prosecution has had an equally rough time finding witnesses willing to testify. The reason in both cases is fear of retaliation at the hands of minions of the jailed Edmond.

Nor is the fear groundless. At least one government informant in the cocaine conspiracy case against Edmond was shot earlier this year and later found with her mouth taped shut and apparently suffering from a drug overdose. And just the other day, the home of the mother of a key prosecution witness was firebombed.

Now it may be that the Edmond organization, which police believe is responsible for dozens of drug-related murders in the Washington area, is so aberrationally violent that we shouldn't even try to extrapolate from it.

But it may be more accurate to conclude that, given the stupendous amounts of money to be made in the drug traffic, Edmond stands as a warning of things to come.

Indeed it could get a lot worse. Americans look with some mix of pity and Yankee superiority at what drug-financed terrorists are doing to the governments of Central and South America. Colombia's minister of justice, Monica de Greiff, has quit her post following weeks of death threats from drug traffickers, one of whom threatened to decapitate her 3-year-old son. She was Colombia's eighth justice minister in just three years. One of her predecessors was murdered.

Peru fears that joining in the U.S. war on drugs could further impoverish its peasant farmers and swell the ranks of subversives.

And some believe that the U.S. drug indictment against Panama's Gen. Noriega is one of the reasons he insists on clinging to power, even after losing an election.

Is it farfetched to believe that American drug kingpins, who have shown no reluctance to ordering "hits" on informants and prosecution witnesses, would balk at taking out a judge?

And is it impossible to imagine that at least some American law-enforcement agents and, yes, judges, might see their way clear to looking the other way or finding legal technicalities on which to release drug defendants if the alternative is a futile martyrdom?

We are a long way from the state of affairs where drug traffickers are offering the grim choice of *plata a plomo*—silver or lead—which is to say, accept a bribe or be killed. But is it out of the question that we could get there?

The sobering thought is that these problems, actual and potential, may represent a greater danger to our national well-being than the prospect of even the few thousand additional zonked-out druggies that legalization might or might not produce.

Schmoke's notion is that we ought to separate the public-health problems of drug abuse from the public-safety problems of antidrug enforcement.

He thinks that it might be wise to decriminalize drugs, thereby depriving the traffickers of the hideous profits that make assassination an acceptable aspect of their business. With the profits gone, and the necessity of budget-straining enforcement disposed of, he argues, we could then devote additional resources to prevention and treatment of drug abuse.

He hasn't persuaded me yet, but his argument is making more and more sense.

(October 1989)

PUTTING AN EX-CONVICT

OUT OF WORK

AARON WILLIAMS' REASONING seemed impeccable. As long as he was going to be doing 10 years in the slammer, he might as well spend the time improving his mind and his post-prison job prospects.

And so for five years at the federal prison in Atlanta and another five in Lewisburg, he took every course he could get into: Arabic, barbering, small business management, dental technology, heating and air-conditioning, carpet laying and even something called "coping." A junior high dropout testing at the 4th grade level when he went in, he left prison with the equivalent of almost four years of college credits.

He's been out on parole for three months now, and for the last couple of weeks, he's been out of work. He's only moderately frustrated that he has been unable to find work in the areas he trained for. His real frustration is that he was forced to quit the one job he did find. His probation officer made him do it.

Rudolph Yates, who runs a program called Efforts from Ex-Convicts (EFEC), had found Williams a job in a halfway house run by the agency. The hours were terrible (he worked a two-man midnight-to-8 a.m. shift, keeping track of residents as they returned from passes, doing security checks and reporting problems to the day shift). But the pay—$10,500 a year—and the prospects for advancement held the hope of transforming him from a family liability into a reliable breadwinner.

The job lasted four days. On the fifth day, his parole officer, Paul Dipolito, invoked Clause No. 10 of the certificate of parole that federal prisoners must sign as a condition of their release: "You shall not associate with persons who have a criminal record unless you have permission of your probation officer."

There's no question that his EFEC job brought him into association with persons with criminal records. But, given his own record of self-rehabilitation, he thought he would have no problem getting permission to continue his work. He was wrong. Dipolito said no, and an appeal to the regional parole office in Philadelphia brought no relief.

As a result, the 37-year-old Williams is out of work and on the brink of losing the car that would help him expand his now-desperate job search into the suburbs.

Yates said it wasn't charity that prompted him to hire Williams at the halfway house. "Based on my interview with him, his educational accomplishments and the glowing letters from prison officials, I thought he could be extremely useful to our organization as a kind of role model.

"As I understand it, the rule is designed to keep parolees from hanging around dives and seedy pool halls—not to keep a man from taking a legitimate job. You know what I think? I think the probation officer went off half-cocked and made a misjudgment, and the bureaucracy has its back up and won't try to be flexible."

If there is an alternative explanation, you can't get it from Dipolito, who says, "The only response I can give you is that I can't give you a response." Daniel P. Lopez, regional probation commissioner in Philadelphia, said he was "inclined to go along with the probation agent, based on my personal experience. . . . This is a job that would be detrimental to this young man."

"It's a silly decision," says Williams, who spent much of his in-prison time teaching Arabic and the Islamic religion. "Every time I go somewhere—the 7-Eleven, the movies, the market or downtown—I see ex-cons. You've got so many blacks in D.C. who have been locked up, it's impossible not to come in contact with ex-cons. But the point is, they don't influence me; I influence them. I don't smoke or drink or do drugs. I don't need nobody to help me do bad. In fact, I have helped a lot of people straighten out. Check my record."

But Williams' in-prison record isn't at issue. The issue is the senseless insistence on stretching a questionable rule (the D.C. parole board dropped it some years ago) to the point of silliness.

It's hard enough for an ex-convict to get a decent job, and harder still to stay straight without a job. By what logic does it make sense for a government agency—established to help ex-offenders re-enter society—to go out of its way to turn a rehabilitated man into a jobless bum?

(May 1986)

LAW AND ORDER IS

PART OF THE PROBLEM

THERE'S A CERTAIN UNDENIABLE TRUTH in the aphorism, attributed to Philadephia's Frank Rizzo, that a conservative is a liberal who has been mugged.

Well, what do you call a conservative who has been hit over the head by the realization that his hard-nosed, no-nonsense approach isn't working, either, and may even be exacerbating the problem?

When it comes to the question of crime and punishment, we may wind up calling him a "progressive."

Like Charles Colson, the former Nixon aide who did time for Watergate offenses and who now is pitching for alternative, nonprison sentencing.

To understand the problem, you need look no further than a report released yesterday by the National Council on Crime and Delinquency. The San Francisco-based think tank begins by telling us what has happened to our prison populations. In 1850, we had an incarceration rate of only 29 inmates per

100,000 population. A short time later, the rate climbed to nearly 100 inmates per 100,000 population, and there it stayed—between 75 and 125 per 100,000—until about 1970.

Since then, it has doubled, and the trend shows no sign of abating. The past decade, in fact, has seen the greatest increase in incarceration rates in the history of the United States. Prisons everywhere are overcrowded and dangerous, and the cost of building new cells to accommodate the court-ordered reductions in overcrowding is increasingly prohibitive. That's one of the reasons for Colson's recent interest in restitution and other nonprison alternatives.

The interesting thing, though, is what is causing the growth. It is, in a word, conservatism: the hardheaded, no-nonsense approach to crime.

"We are sending more people to prison for longer periods of time," James Austin, NCCD's director of research, said in a telephone interview.

"Longer sentences create what is called a 'stacking effect.' That is, the prisons become more crowded even if the number of admissions doesn't change."

But hardheaded law enforcement also increases the number of admissions. And when you add the failure of parole—two-thirds of the prison admissions in Oregon and Texas are not for new felonies but for technical violations of parole and probation—you get the overcrowding disaster that is mugging erstwhile conservatives.

Nor is overcrowding the only problem of "no-nonsense" law enforcement. Says Austin: "The problem has a tremendous impact on state services. California (with 67,000 prisoners and the national leader in prison population growth) has a prison budget of $1.6 billion a year. When the prison population reaches 100,000, as it figures to do in the next five or six years, the cost will be nearly $3 billion. That will take its toll on other state services, including education and medical care, both of which might have a greater impact on the crime problem.

"In addition, the bulk of the growth will be among blacks

and Hispanics, both disproportionately involved in street drug activity, and that will create additional problems.

"And finally, as the prison population gets older—an inevitable result of longer sentences—we will find not only that prisons will need to provide special geriatric services but also that imprisonment will become much less effective in dealing with crime. Crime is a young man's game. But when older offenders, who are not that big a threat anymore, take up more and more prison space, you run out of space for the younger men who are feeding the crime statistics, particularly members of the underclass."

So what would Austin do? He'd turn away from the conservative approach by shortening prison terms to relieve overcrowding and by working to reduce the failure of parole.

"But the bottom line, in terms of the generation coming on, the 10- and 11-year-olds of today, is that we've got to look for something other than building new prisons. That won't make us safer. In California, we've tripled the prison population since 1977, but the crime rate hasn't changed one bit.

"The people who are committing crime are not in prison; they're young men in the street. We're not dealing with the dynamics of the underclass, which is getting larger."

And so Austin winds up with a call not for bigger and better prisons but the need to do something about the causes of crime. He knows it sounds like the old "discredited" liberal position, but that is where the assault of reality seems to lead.

"Trying to solve the crime problem by building more prison cells," he says, "is like trying to solve the problem of AIDS by building more hospitals."

(April 1988)

A Sentence That Says a Lot

THERE YOU ARE AT THE BAR, having downed maybe a couple of drinks more than your limit, when this older woman makes a pass at you. She's not your type, though, and you're so deeply offended that she seems to think otherwise that you and your buddy invite her into your Chevy on the pretext of taking her to a party.

You drive her instead to a deserted park, force her at knife point to strip and lie, spread-eagle, on the ground. Then you rob her and kick her and urinate on her and threaten to kill her. She resists, and during the ensuing struggle, you and your buddy manage to slash her hand, severing four tendons.

She fends you off with a tree limb, then takes off through the park, running for her life. Finally she reaches a neighboring house, where the occupant, hearing the pounding on the door, lets her, naked and bleeding, inside.

You and your buddy are arrested, charged and convicted. What do you think your sentence should be? Would you believe probation and 400 hours of volunteer work in a soup kitchen?

Of course you wouldn't believe it.

Well, suppose you and your buddy were teen-agers, that your victim wasn't a woman but a homosexual man, and that the sentencing judge was Nicholas Nunzio.

Do I hear you saying that that shouldn't make any difference? Wrong again. The judge, "satisfied that the case [was] one of excessive alcohol use, . . . of a sexual advance on the part of the complaining witness, and of excessive force in the defense of that sexual advance," treated the whole affair as though it were about as serious as a panty raid.

In fact, the assault may have been a little worse than I have described it here. The victim, a 32-year-old computer consultant named William Hassell, said he never made a sexual advance toward Matthew Warring, 18, and Kevin Kinnahan, 17. The prosecutor's contention was that youngsters had set out that evening last November with the express idea of bashing a gay. But even if it happened the way the teen-agers themselves said it happened, it's hard to understand Nunzio's incredibly light sentence as anything other than a statement that gay-bashing isn't really all that terrible.

The authorities at St. John's College High School, where the convicted youths were students, seemed to share that feeling. Both students were allowed to remain in school between the time of their guilty plea and their sentencing by Nunzio. This is the same school that has put kids on probation for smarting off with teachers and expelled them for stealing. Beating and slashing a man within an inch of his life apparently doesn't warrant even a suspension, if that man is an acknowledged homosexual.

U.S. Attorney Joseph E. diGenova expressed astonishment at the light sentences handed the youngsters, who were put on probation and ordered not to use alcohol until they were 21, at which time their records will be cleared. "The behavior by these kids was barbaric," diGenova said, adding, in world-class understatement, that the sentences were "not commensurate with the gross nature of their conduct."

I don't know what there is about some men (and boys) that leads them to hate homosexuals with such brutal passion. I don't know what makes some of us think that the only proper response to a sexual advance from a homosexual is to punch him out. I don't know why some of us find it easy just to keep walking in the face of an advance from the dirtiest, ugliest, most repulsive wino in the gutter, if the wino is a woman, but go into a violent rage if the advance comes from even the most respectable looking homosexual.

But it isn't the role of the sentencing judge to explain our irrational fears. His job is to punish our violent behavior.

Judge Nunzio didn't do his job, and it isn't just the gay community that ought to be outraged.

(May 1984)

ON FAMILY

PARENTING: A LOST ART?

WHEN ELEANOR HOLMES NORTON, former government official and current Georgetown law professor, was about 6 years old, she remembers, her grandmother sent her to the corner market to purchase three lamb chops.

The two- or three-block trek went smoothly enough (with Grandma watching from the porch as far as she could). "When I got to the store, the man asked me if I wanted those chops over there, and I told him, no, I didn't like the way those looked. 'I'll take these,' I told him.

"When I got home, I told my grandmother about it, and then something marvelous happened. For weeks and weeks after that, she would tell the story to relatives and family friends. 'You know, I sent Eleanor to the store for some lamb chops, and when the man tried to sell her some shriveled-up little chops, she looked him right in the eye and told him, "No I don't want those. I'll take these, thank you."'

"The way she'd tell the story would make me feel like the

smartest, most self-assertive little girl in town. She had an instinct for doing that sort of thing, and I'm certain it is one of the reasons for my self-confidence today."

It reminded me, I told her, of my own mother's notion that, since she knew the world would try to tear us down, her role was to build us up.

Our story-swapping was part of a recent conversation (as most of my "interviews" with her quickly become) on the problems of parenting. It is her belief that too many of us—blacks in particular—have lost the instinct for parenting that many members of her grandmother's generation had. And it is her urgent warning that we had better do something to recapture and improve on it.

Something like this? I shared with her a recent letter from a reader, a convert to Judaism, who said she had been struck by the amount of time and energy Jewish parents devote to conversations with their children.

"Every question is seen as an opportunity to convey knowledge," the letter said. "I think back to my own upbringing in a rather lower-class white society where my mother thought children were to be seen and not heard. Questions were viewed as intrusions into the adult world. As a public health nurse several years back, I can recall that same attitude existed with my black patients. Time and time again black parents missed the opportunity to take their children's questions seriously.

"Even now, I get anxious and can never seem to articulate well enough in a large group to get my point across. My family loved me, but they weren't much interested in what I had to say. Those early experiences seem to stick. My [teenage] children are better than I was, but I didn't start soon enough."

"Brilliant insight!" said Norton, who would like to see some effort on the part of blacks to institutionalize—in public-school classes and elsewhere—such successful child-rearing techniques. "And the wonderful thing is that, as your story and mine indicate, it's nothing that has to be reinvented. We simply need to draw more on the things that are already in our culture."

The former chair of the federal Equal Employment Opportunity Commission, never content to keep a good idea to
herself, already is looking for ways to "get people talking"
about pooling ideas, devising programs and finding ways to
resurrect the folk wisdom that many parents used to have.

Not that we need to copy everything they did. "Even now,
you watch black children in the supermarket doing the things
that children naturally do, and their parents will often threaten
to hit them if they don't stop. I understand that there was a
time when such childish behavior could have gotten both the
child and the parent in trouble. But the point is that by being
too careful we can kill their natural curiosity.

"Still, the old folk, uneducated as they often were, did a lot
of things that were right. They understood what we have to
make our young mothers in particular understand: that love is
not enough."

(March 1985)

Teaching the Parents

No one thing can fix everything, and anyone who tells you otherwise is trying to sell you something.

Let me try to sell you something that won't fix everything but might make a lot of our problems a little easier to handle. Let me try to sell you the idea of teaching parents how to be parents.

I don't have to convince you that too many of our youngsters are falling into the category we have lately started labeling "at risk." Not just the sexually careless adolescents, the high school dropouts or the teenage hustlers, who are, admittedly, easier to worry about than to set straight. I'm thinking about the 6-year-olds starting school in a few weeks who will be "at risk" from their first day in first grade, their younger siblings who will be "at risk" even in preschool and kindergarten, the babies who are in fact born "at risk."

The notion I'm trying to sell is that a lot of that risk could be avoided by the simple device of teaching the parents of these ill-fated children how to get them ready for learning, how to develop in them the attitudes and habits that will give them a decent chance at success—how to be good parents.

I'm not talking about the tough cases: the crack babies who may be permanently damaged by their parents' drug abuse, the abandoned infants languishing in the foster care system or the abused and brutalized children who have never known a parent's love. I'm talking about the children whose parents love them and want the best for them but simply don't know how to give the best a chance to happen.

I'm proposing that we teach them how.

Parental love is as natural as rain. Parenting *skills* have to be learned. That simple truth often escapes those of us in the middle class who consider ourselves pretty good at the parenting game although we don't remember anyone teaching us how to do it.

Well, someone did. We learned what we know about parenting from our own parents, and in most cases it serves us pretty well. But an awful lot of young parents—themselves the children of teenage mothers, half-formed families and unskilled parents—don't know what we know.

They love their children, and they will sacrifice their own interests in order to buy them expensive toys and dress them in cute clothes. But they don't know how to get them ready for learning or for life.

Interestingly enough, there are people who are expert in teaching these things: child psychologists, early childhood educators and people like Dorothy Rich, of the Washington-based Home and School Institute, who has made a career of teaching parents how to give their children the skills and attitudes that make for school success. I suspect that there are few school districts in America that don't have access to some of these experts.

What is lacking is any routine way of drawing on their expertise. We need to have parenting centers in every city and hamlet, places where parents can go, without charge, to learn how to get their children off to a good start. We need to teach them the importance of reading to their children, talking to them, teaching them not just such "academic" skills as color and shape and letters but also self-confidence, perseverance and personal responsibility—the things that make school learning possible.

It wouldn't solve the problem of poverty, though it would make it more likely that the next generation would have the skills and attitudes to help escape poverty. It wouldn't cure adolescent pregnancy, but it might help a lot of youngsters to have the confidence in the future that makes postponing pregnancy seem worthwhile. It wouldn't eliminate the scourge of drugs, but it might strengthen a lot of children to resist the lure of drugs. It wouldn't eliminate the need for school reform, but it would give at-risk youngsters a far better chance at school success.

We need to start thinking of our children—all our children—as a national resource, and of their academic, emotional and moral health as a national priority. The children need a better chance, and we who talk so much about national "competitiveness" and changing demographics need them to have that better chance.

And, no, I'm not talking about putting another burden on an already overburdened school system. It wouldn't matter whether the centers I am advocating are run by schools, by churches or by local civic groups; the problem affects the entire community, and the entire community ought to be involved in its solution.

(August 1990)

LAP TIME

OKAY, I'M SKEPTICAL OF PAT THEORIES, TOO—especially when they promise more than seems reasonable to expect. But if you can suspend your skepticism for a few minutes, you just might find yourself nodding in agreement as Frances Cress Welsing spins out her theory of what has gone wrong with America's children. The problem, says this controversial Washington psychiatrist, is: Too little "lap time."

She is talking about the thing you have observed, and perhaps experienced. A child wants to be held, and the mother responds. "If she's relaxed about it, the child will get into a state of deep relaxation, and then, after a while, will say 'Let me down.' Children know when they've had enough." The problem, she says, is that too many of our children—black children in particular—don't get enough at the appropriate age, and the dearth of lap time later propels them into premature sex, alcohol and drug abuse: "What we are experiencing [in drug abuse and adolescent sex] is an epidemic of dependency deprivation among our group."

It's an age-old problem, she says, which perpetuates itself because we tend to learn our parenting styles from our own parents. "Imagine what it was like to be a black baby in slavery. A child cries and cries and cries, but the mother, having work to do, can't pick it up and give it the attention it needs. So the child grows up and becomes a parent without having learned how to satisfy emotional needs, and so it is passed on. After slavery, given the fact that women found it necessary to function as breadwinners because the men were often denied the opportunity to work, we ended up with overwhelmed mothers who didn't have the time or emotional energy to provide an adequate amount of lap time for their children, who, in addition, may have been too closely spaced."

While Welsing's emphasis is on black children, she insists that her theory applies with equal force to white children. "This culture has attempted to substitute material things for emotional needs, and it doesn't work. And as a result, even children from well-to-do families are getting into all kinds of trouble with drugs and sex. Orientals, on the other hand, tend to give their children a great deal of lap time, and, as a result, they have the lowest rates of crimes and adolescent pregnancy and the other things that are plaguing us."

She says she is constantly struck by how often, both in her clinical practice and in her frequent visits to schools, the answer comes back "no" when she asks teen-agers if they got enough lap time when they were growing up.

For the younger ones, she says, she tries to counsel the children to communicate their need for affection and their parents to provide it. For the older ones, she tries to help them understand that they can learn to "be good to themselves—no calling yourself names and all that." But there really is no substitute for lap time, she insists.

Perhaps she would like to offer some sort of caveat, lest those who hear her conclude that she believes that adequate "lap time" would eliminate all social problems?

Well, not really. "We will be well into the prevention of all the things we call social ills if we understand the critical importance of adequate emotional nurturing.... So much of what we see as social problems is really a search for something to kill the pain of longing, of not feeling validated and loved"—of inadequate "lap time."

(October 1986)

CHILDREN OF THE STREETS

SO FAR AS I KNOW, William Golding, the British author, never visited—probably never even thought about—the violence-wracked inner cities of America.

And yet, when I think about what is happening in so many places—emphatically including Detroit, where black teenagers are shooting each other at the appalling rate of nearly one a day—I find myself reflecting on a theme that runs through practically all the 76-year-old Golding's fiction.

The theme is this: the moral order we call civilization is a delicate, skin-deep thing that, left untended, peels away to expose us for the amoral savages we really are.

Is that what is happening in our inner cities?

In *Lord of the Flies*, which Golding wrote some 32 years ago, a group of English schoolboys crash-lands on a deserted island. The adults are killed, and the youngsters, despairing of rescue, set out to build their own society. At first, the older boys try to draw on their memory of English society; but they don't remember enough, and there are no experienced elders to whom they can turn for guidance.

The book is the story of their descent—inevitable, as Golding saw it—into savagery, paganism, terror and blood sacrifice. Adult supervision might have saved them, but the adults weren't there.

If Golding could believe that a group of well-bred British boys, children of wealth and privilege, could so quickly shed the veneer of civilization, I can believe it of children born to no privilege at all.

I don't mean simply that inner-city children are, virtually by definition, poor. The problem is not money but values, and values have to be taught and (as Golding reminds) reinforced over and over again. That is what fails to happen for so many children of the underclass—especially the boys.

I think particularly of the sons of adolescent mothers. These young mothers may love their boys and may try as hard as they know how to raise them straight. But, being mere children themselves, and school dropouts at that, they often lack the skill and patience and wisdom to do a proper job.

Even the brightest of these child-mothers are likely to find that their sons quickly come to resist the civilizing influence of the females in their lives. They are *beset* by females—their mothers, their grandmothers, their teachers—and often bereft of the positive guidance of adult males. The ever-present women may do a reasonably good job of teaching young girls how to be women, but who is to initiate the young boys in the mysteries of manhood? The answer, too often, is: the street.

And it gets worse. Even the good boys, as Golding saw, may find it all but impossible (in the absence of positive male adults) to resist the peer pressure that urges them into such "macho" displays as defiance, truancy and crime. And far too often, even the distant role models—whether politicians or money-grubbing evangelists—reveal that they too are interested primarily in "getting over."

Left to these baleful influences, the boys often don't stand a chance. The values that should guide their behavior never become internalized. Their inner moral compass never fully develops, and they fall prey to unimaginable, conscienceless savagery. It's hard to imagine Detroit's young gunmen tossing, conscience-stricken, at night, thinking: I've shot someone.

Golding leaves us on a positive note. A tall, strong naval officer finally finds them. And though it may be too late to save them all, we are left with the hope that at least some of the boys will be salvaged.

In the case of the American slums, the role of the rescuing naval officer must fall, if only by default, to the strong black men of the black middle class. We have to go searching for these luckless children and save those who still can be saved, for society's sake as well as for their own.

And, yes: the whole community must do what it can to eliminate the thoroughly foreseeable "accidents" that threaten to produce another generation of young castaways.

(May 1987)

BRING BACK THE FAMILY

IF I COULD OFFER a single prescription for the survival of America, and particularly of black America, it would be: restore the family.

And if you asked me how to do it, my answer—doubtless oversimplified—would be: save the boys.

So much of what has gone wrong in America, including the frightening growth of the poverty-stricken, crime-ridden and despairing black underclass, can be traced to the disintegration of the family structure.

Everybody knows it, but too many have been reluctant to talk straight about it. We know that children need intact families that include fathers, but we fear to say it lest we appear to be blaming hard-pressed single mothers for the very problems they are struggling to overcome.

The point, however, is not to assign blame but to encourage analysis that can lead the way to solutions. And we are not likely to undertake that analysis so long as we persist in talking about the explosion of female-headed households as a mere change in lifestyle, away from the old-fashioned "Ozzie and Harriet" model to new arrangements in which two-parent families represent merely another option.

Nathan and Julia Hare put it this way in their book, *The Endangered Black Family*:

"There is nothing wrong with being a black female single-parent—and one rightfully makes the most of any situation in which she/he finds herself. But there is something wrong with *why* a black woman is so much more likely to experience the single-parent situation, why one race can freely imprison, send off to military duty, unemploy, underemploy and otherwise destroy the oppressed black woman's eligible male supply.

"Also, there is something wrong with glorifying this problem instead of rising up to change it. People will speak here of 'options,' but forced or unintended options must be called by some other name."

That's from a pair of radical black social scientists. Now hear this from white ethologist Phon Hudkins:

"The family is the only social institution that is present in every single village, tribe, or nation we know through history. It has a genetic base and is the rearing device for our species."

Or the conservative Richard John Neuhaus, editor of the *Religion & Society Report*:

"Millions of children do not know, and will never know, what it means to have a father. More poignantly, they do not know anyone who has a father or is a father.... It takes little imagination to begin to understand the intergenerational consequences of this situation. It is reasonable to ask whether, in all of human history, we have an instance of a large population in which the institution of the family simply disappeared. It is reasonable and ominous, for the answer is almost certainly no. There is no historical precedent supporting the hope that the family, once it has disappeared, can be reconstituted."

It strikes me as it strikes these writers—as it struck Daniel Patrick Moynihan a quarter century ago—that children unlucky enough to be born into single-parent households are, if not doomed, at least at serious disadvantage.

Hudkins believes the disadvantages include not just poverty and crime and hopelessness but also poor health produced by the stress of familylessness.

This stress, he says, "suppresses the immune response, making people susceptible to a host of physical and nervous and mental diseases like cancer, in addition to uncontrolled aggression."

The question is what to do about the children of deteriorating and never-formed families. The first thing to do, it seems to me, is to provide as much help as we can for these feckless children in their present circumstances: education, mentoring, role-modeling, job training, help toward self-sufficiency. The second is to devise policies to restore families.

Hudkins, who has been ridiculed for his contention that female dominance is eroding America's strength, has it right in the prescription he offered in a recent open letter to the president:

"If families are to be formed and survive, young males must be prepared for skilled jobs to support these families. In order to do this, we must target our government aid and our compensatory education and training programs for disadvantaged young males."

We can't rescue America's families unless we make up our minds to save the boys.

(July 1989)

(Middle) Class Struggle

There was never a good time to be poor, but the years just ahead may be worse than most.

America's black leadership (which is just about the only organized advocacy there is for the poor) is still making demands on the society for a better shake for bottom-of-the-barrel America. But the demands seem more modest than in the past, and the demanders less hopeful.

The talk these days is not of "domestic Marshall Plans" for America's poor, of major new outlays to lift the poor out of their poverty. The 1980 optimist is the guy who hopes that programs for the poor won't be cut back too severely.

But if there are mean times ahead for the poor, it isn't because America has turned mean. It is because middle-income America—the segment of the population that pays the bills for our social programs—is itself in trouble, struggling for its own economic survival.

It's hard, under such circumstances, to evoke charitable feelings for those who are even worse off.

One resident of Southeast Washington—a black woman—says it with more feeling (and far more candor) than you are likely to hear from any black leader or from any candidate for public office.

"I am a single parent who has traveled the bootstrap route, and I now earn over $25,000 a year," she told me. "Because I have no mortgage interest or property taxes to write off, I pay the maximum in both local and federal income taxes: 11 percent and 36 percent respectively.

"Mandatory retirement deductions of 7 percent leave me with 46 percent of my earnings. On top of that, I have been hit by increased rent and energy costs as well as the other forms of inflation. Saving money for a down payment on a home—or anything else, for that matter—has become increasingly difficult. Besides, it is clear that even if I manage to acquire a down payment of X amount, the required amount will always be X-plus.

"Yet all of the home-ownership programs exclude me because I earn too much money. My tax dollars enable others to own their own homes, including people who haven't the foggiest notion of home-ownership responsibility and who have not sacrificed in order to buy."

She knows the importance of home ownership, even for low-income families. She knows that poor people need special help. But considering her own tight situation—even at $25,000 a year—she doesn't think she should be called upon to provide that special help.

You could, I suppose, accuse her of having made it up from poverty only to turn her back on those she left behind. But don't expect her to accept the charge. From her point of view, she is hanging on to her hard-won middle-class status by her fingernails. To ask her to reach out a helping hand to someone else is to ask her to fall back into the pit of poverty.

It is this attitude—this fear—on the part of middle-class

America, black and white, that is rendering so unpopular the demands that more and more be done for the poor.

It isn't hardheartedness that accounts for the present attitude. No one relishes the idea of hungry children, of families living in squalor and despair. It is the perception among the middle class that they themselves are in trouble and that nobody seems to give a damn.

And what would my Southeast Washington correspondent, who has known poverty firsthand, do about those who are still poor?

I don't know. But I suspect that she, like her middle-class counterparts across the land, would see gainful employment as the only reasonable solution.

But jobs programs of the sort generally advocated cost tax dollars, too. The fact is that nothing is going to get better for those at or near the bottom of the barrel until something is done to repair the American economy, to break the inflation that is strangling us all to death.

And nobody—neither the black leadership, the politicians, the economists nor the victims of the deteriorating economy—seems to have any solid idea of how to do it.

(March 1980)

THE DRUG WAR WILL BE WON

ON THE HOME FRONT

WHEN THEY WRITE THE STORY of how this city finally won its war against drugs, don't expect it to be told in tons of drugs interdicted or of major distribution centers smashed or of drug kingpins hauled off to prison.

It's far more likely that the story will record the success of a grass-roots effort, beginning in earnest in the early months of 1988, when hundreds of ordinary people decided that they were mad as hell and weren't going to take it any more.

This isn't what President Reagan had in mind when he said the other day that the "tide has turned" in the drug war.

It may be that war is a misleading analogy to begin with. Surely the scourge of drugs has some of the attributes of international war. But it also has some of the qualities of a deadly epidemic, some of the qualities of a crime wave and some of the qualities of—well, sin.

Despite the president's optimism, the fight isn't going well at the level of international war. We may know the countries from which the invading armies come, and even the names of some of the most dangerous generals: Panama's Manuel Noriega, for instance, whose indictment for drug trafficking has done more to destabilize Panama than to staunch the flow of killer drugs to America.

That is true, in part, because drug trafficking is a peculiar form of war; its assaults are effective only through the cooperation of the intended victims. As long as that cooperation exists—as long as there is a demand for drugs and huge sums of money to be made from supplying that demand—there will be suppliers and ways for them to penetrate our defenses.

We also need to act on the health problem that drug abuse represents. Indeed, building new drug treatment facilities may prove more effective, against ordinary street crime as well as against drug trafficking specifically, than putting the same money into new prison cells.

But for me, the most encouraging news is what is happening in some of this city's most drug-ridden neighborhoods. Worried parents and preachers, vulnerable teen-agers and concerned community leaders have declared their own war on drugs. They have served notice that they will no longer tolerate the infiltration of pushers into their communities. They have pledged to help police close down "crack houses" and other places known to be dealing drugs.

They won't argue with the president's pledge to do something about the international menace of drug dealing, but they recognize their own need to do something about the enemy agent nearer at hand: the big-spending dealer bent on recruiting or poisoning their children.

And also to do something about their children. Intellectuals may ascribe all manner of psychological motives to Lonise Bias' national crusade to educate young people on the evil of the drugs that claimed the life of her superstar son Len. Sophisticates may titter at Nancy Reagan's exhortation to "Just say no."

But some Washington parents are coming to realize that no amount of law-enforcement vigilance can protect their children from drugs unless the children themselves have been taught the necessity of resistance.

It goes even beyond that. As Eric Knight, the suspended football coach at Forestville High School, told a gathering of the school's seniors (after the drug-induced death of a star athlete), girls who accept expensive gifts from boys only encourage them to hustle drugs. Catholics used to call it the "near occasion of sin"—the person or agent who tempts someone into sin.

That quaint category must surely include the mothers who accept cash and clothing from their teen-age sons, taking care not to ask where the money comes from. But even without asking, they know; it comes from the same evil source that already has cost the lives of some three dozen D.C. residents so far this year.

Certainly the war on drugs must be fought by federal, state and local agencies. But it must be fought on the neighborhood and personal levels as well.

That is what a small army of local Washingtonians has started to do. Can they win? I don't know. They are fighting a powerful, and powerfully financed, enemy. But if the rest of us will join their homefront effort, I think we've got a chance.

Indeed, it may be the only chance we have.

(March 1988)

WELFARE'S LIMITS

I HAVE LOST COUNT of the number of welfare-reform proposals under consideration by Congress or being urged on it by one expert group or another. What sticks in my mind, aside from the fact that virtually all of them have some provision for "workfare," is that none of them can work.

I don't suggest that there is no reason why particular "reformers" might not prefer one proposal to the others, or even that requiring some work in exchange for a welfare check (provided there is adequate day-care, health insurance, protection against coerced drudgery, etc., etc.) is bad.

When I say that none of the proposals can work, I have in mind the one thing that all the reformers would like to accomplish: a system that gives money to those families that desperately need it while encouraging the able-bodied to work.

The dilemma is familiar enough. Make the welfare grant large enough to permit a family to live in decency and you make it foolish for potential grantees to take low-paying jobs.

Make it small enough to render bottom-of-the-barrel jobs attractive, and you guarantee that the jobless will live in squalor. Subsidize the lowest-paid jobs and you have to subsidize the jobs at the next higher level; how can you pay the assistant janitor and the janitor the same salary?

How do you get out of that conundrum? The short answer is: You can't. No amount of tinkering with welfare rules will solve the fundamental dilemma. If you are comparing the current welfare grant with wages from the current available bottom-rung job, the grant (taking into account automatic eligibility for free medical care) will either be big enough to make the job seem a bad bargain or too small to afford a decent existence for those unable to land even a bad job.

Indeed, the problem would be a great deal worse if poor people were cleverer at computing the relative benefits. As it is, thousands of poor parents toil away at awful jobs when they would be better off economically to quit and go on welfare.

But there are reasons aside from mathematical ineptness to prefer even a dreadful job to welfare. One reason is simple pride. There are people (though fewer, I suspect, than before the 1960s Welfare Rights Movement) who find being on the public dole so humiliating that they will take almost any kind of job to avoid it.

But there is another reason that has been given too little stress. Work and welfare, no matter how comparable their initial benefits, have an important distinction. You cannot get good at welfare. It does no good for a welfare mother to impress her case worker with her quick grasp or her sense of responsibility or her willingness to take on an extra task. There is no way for a welfare client to distinguish himself, in any economically useful way, from any other welfare client. There are no promotions on welfare.

Even the worst-paid jobs provide the opportunity for résumé-building. The work may be mindless drudgery, with no possibility of promotion. But a worker still can demonstrate such qualities as reliability, honesty, punctuality—things that could make him more attractive to another employer who might be able to offer better opportunities for promotion.

This is emphatically not to say that the poor have only themselves and their poor attitudes to blame for their joblessness and poverty. There have been periods in American history when virtually any adult with a willingness to work could find a decent job. There have also been periods when well-qualified people found it impossible to secure regular work. And there have been times and places—including today in the urban ghettos—when the marginally qualified have trouble finding work.

The *societal* problem of poverty and joblessness cannot be solved until the problems with the American economy are solved. But even in the present circumstances, individuals can do a great deal about their individual plight. Even in areas where unemployment rates reach 50 percent, half the people are working. We can do a good deal more than we are doing to teach people how to place themselves among the half that's working. We can teach them about the value of correct attitudes, and hold up examples of where correct attitudes have paid off.

But you can't do it with welfare reform. No formula, no matter how cleverly concocted, can avoid the dilemma of disincentives to low-paid work on the one hand or governmentally enforced squalor on the other.

The only way out of that problem, pending major improvements in the economy and the skill levels of job seekers, lies in teaching—and consciously rewarding—the necessary attitudes.

(April 1988)

WELFARE WONDERLAND

THERE'S ANOTHER DILEMMA to the business of welfare. The first, which I discussed in a recent column, is that if welfare grants are set at levels high enough to provide elemental decency for recipients, they become a disincentive to work. And if they are low enough to encourage recipients to take even low-paid work, they condemn to squalor those who do not manage to find work in our job-poor economy.

The other dilemma is this: present rules, which link payments to the number of children, do nothing to encourage family planning, with the result that many welfare families have so many children that it is impossible—money aside—to take decent care of any of them. But to break the link between size of family and size of check is to punish innocent children.

It is true that this aspect of the welfare program is not quite the fiscal ogre it's generally perceived to be. Of the total federal outlays for welfare assistance, only about half—$5.8 billion last year—is for Aid to Families with Dependent Children, while the other half—$5.5 billion in fiscal '79—is for the Supplemental Security Income for the aged, the blind and the disabled.

But this is of little consequence to critics of the system. Listen to one of the critics, a solid liberal with a record of genuine concern for the poor—especially poor children:

"The aged, crippled and otherwise handicapped are, so to speak, dead-end groups, finite and self-limiting. Only the welfare mothers-of-many are engaged in compounding, multiplying and exacerbating the problem they represent—and being paid to do so. And any thoughtful person can get good and tired of hearing the everlasting: 'But they don't have all those babies on *purpose* in order to increase their monthly payments.'

"Certainly most of them *don't* have all those babies on purpose. Having babies requires no purpose. *Not* having babies is what has to be done on purpose.

"The hard-core [often second- or third-generation] welfare mothers live in an alien and alienated world of their own, a Wonderland in which things operate in reverse. And the payment-per-baby has to be the most topsy-turvy reversal of them all.

"The bricklayer with eight children does not automatically receive six times as much per hour as the bricklayer with one child. The typist with two children is not entitled, no questions asked, to twice the salary of a childless co-worker at the next typewriter. In the real world, each additional child means spreading the family income just a bit thinner—stretching, contriving, thinking ahead—an obvious incentive to family planning, and a pretty vivid disincentive to just letting nature take its course.

"Nobody in the real world claims that this is a punishment imposed by a heartless authority. It is simply a fact of life, the impersonal operation of the law of cause and effect."

Indeed, says this liberal, this disjunction from the real world is the main reason why welfare tends to entrap its beneficiaries into permanent dependency.

Nor is it just the fact that this dependency is a burden to taxpayers.

"If the problem were money," says the liberal, "we should shoot the admiral or general on the prowl for a few more billions in explosive hardware. The problem is people—the poor little waifs born a half-mile behind the starting line, and shoved further backward with the birth of each younger sibling."

Few candid social workers, and fewer teachers in low-income schools, would disagree with that assessment. But how do you set things right without extracting the price from the very children whose welfare is the primary concern?

"If it were possible to start over from scratch," says the liberal, "I would vote to promote the inhabitants of Wonderland into the real world. I would offer each girl, on the birth of her first 'fatherless' baby, a guaranteed income sufficient to bring up one child in decency and comfort.

"But after the first child, there would be no raises in pay (except perhaps a cost-of-living adjustment)—just the way it works for the real people who have managed not to plunge down the rabbit hole.

"Here is impersonal incentive: to get acquainted with the law of cause and effect and the facts of life; to think ahead; to do something pretty basic *on purpose*, for a change.

"I think most of them would manage. It is not that they are stupid, just that they have never had occasion to use what intelligence they possess and have, in fact, been paid not to use it."

It gets tougher every day to tell the liberals from the conservatives.

(February 1980)

POVERTY, "RESHUFFLED"

JUST WHEN EVERYBODY is starting to understand the "feminization of poverty"—the crucial link between family break-up and poverty—along comes Mary Jo Banes to tell us it ain't necessarily so.

It used to be. Between 1960 and the late 1970s, among both blacks and whites, family-structure changes served to keep the poverty rate higher than it otherwise would have been.

It's not true now. Family-composition changes "contributed almost nothing" to the sharp increase in poverty since 1979.

Bane, executive deputy commissioner of the New York State Department of Social Services, told a recent congressional hearing that she was surprised by her own research findings—so surprised, in fact, that she did further analysis. What she found was an unexpected distinction between "event-caused" poverty among whites and "reshuffled" poverty among blacks.

That is, while three-fourths of poor, female-headed, white

families became poor as a result of the family break-up, two thirds of the poor, female-headed, black families had been poor before their families broke up.

At least among blacks, the frequently remarked increase in the number of poor families does not necessarily reflect an increase in the number of poor individuals. The jobless man who leaves his wife and children increases the number of poor families by one, but leaves the number of poor individuals unchanged.

This is no debate over angels and pinheads. A crucial part of what is coming to be conventional wisdom is the Charles Murray message that the availability of public welfare induces marriage break-ups and out-of-wedlock births and, thereby, adds to poverty. What Bane found is that welfare has no discernible effect on birthrates to unmarried women, but does influence the decision of whether the young mother will live separately from her own parents, thereby increasing the number of poor families, though not the amount of poverty.

The public-policy implications are obvious. If welfare somehow "causes" poverty, then it may make sense to change or even reduce availability of welfare. But if Bane is correct in her belief that the increase in the number of poor families is, to a substantial degree, the result of "reshuffling," then we have to look elsewhere for poverty's basic causes.

Bane says she has found one. "The decline in real benefits levels since the mid-1970s has been an important contributor to poverty among female-headed families, and to their increasing poverty rates since 1979. I have found nothing in my research that would suggest that raising welfare-benefit levels would do anything to make things worse, and much to suggest that raising them would make things better."

She is not suggesting that adolescent pregnancy is other than what it is: a growing disaster that is "ruining innumerable lives among both white and black young women and severely limiting the opportunities available to their children." Nor is she saying that the preservation of the family is of no societal concern, or that welfare ought to be more than an economic

Band-Aid, with increased educational and employment opportunity the only long-term solution. She is only urging that we not let unsound analysis lead us to faulty policy choices.

The family-disintegration idea, she believes, is an appealing but false explanation that may serve to lead us away from the deeply rooted—and worsening—poverty that is besetting a growing segment of our society.

(October 1985)

WELFARE SYSTEMS REQUIRE FAILURE

FOR THEIR OWN SUCCESS

TALK TO SHARON MORRIS-BILOTTI—or better yet, read the series of papers she has written for the Illinois State Department of Children and Family Services—and you're likely to come away thinking about social-service delivery in entirely new ways.

She will tell you, for instance, that different kinds of services expand or contract in quite different ways. School systems ebb and flow depending only on the number of school-age children, independent of their success in teaching the children. The growth of health systems is dependent on their success: People seek medical care only to the extent they believe it will help them.

Welfare systems, however, are unique. They grow in direct proportion to their failure to accomplish their mission: to enhance the life conditions, productivity, skills and self-worth of the people they are supposed to help.

"The more successful the social service is in empowering its consumers, the less likely they are to remain dependent on the system," Morris-Bilotti contends. "The fewer co-dependents we have, the more difficult it will be to finesse an expansion of the system.

"And systems that don't expand tend to lose credibility and power and ultimately receive a smaller proportion of the service dollars."

In short, welfare systems as presently constituted require failure for their own success.

This is not some smart-aleck social critic taking potshots at hard-pressed social workers. Morris-Bilotti has been with the Illinois public welfare system for nearly 30 years. She speaks as an insider, albeit a particularly insightful insider.

Her iconoclastic thoughts are the direct result of her decision to think seriously (and to get her colleagues thinking seriously) about the newest buzzword in her field: empowerment.

"If we are honest," she says, "those of us who have found our way into the provider side of social services know that we need a continuing flow of people who need us.... Yet the nagging little voice of our professional ethic keeps telling us that to continue to suppress America's underclass, to foster their dependency, to render them powerless over their own lives, is the antithesis of empowerment."

The most obvious way of empowering the poor would be to give them the money that now goes to the agencies instituted for their care.

But as Morris-Bilotti notes, there are other means of empowerment: information, access, opportunity, decision-making and so on.

And yet the welfare systems have been loath to share those forms of power as well. Says Morris-Bilotti:

"We have put together a human service system that is so complicated we now need college-educated, specially trained staff who spend months and years trying to figure out and piece together the services and requirements of the multitudinous, multidisciplinary, categorical programs our consumers 'fit into.' We must find the service, make the referrals, run interference, assure funding, and sometimes figure out how to get the consumer to the service. We have even labeled these helpful people 'case managers.'

"Shouldn't that tell us something? Special people to manage the services and resources needed by the consumer, and ultimately their lives, because we have created such a rat maze that no one but a pro can get through it. How can the underclass possibly escape dependency? How can they ever extricate themselves from our help?"

Part of it is rules. Consider: An AFDC mother who scrimps and saves to put aside $3,000 so her daughter can go to college and escape the dependency trap will not be praised for her self-discipline and resourcefulness. She's more likely to find herself convicted of fraud and terminated from the system.

Or this: "Enormous amounts of federal (child welfare) money are available, but states can only access them if they fail to preserve and reunite families—despite the fact that family preservation and reunification are two of the federal government's current buzzwords." (Reimbursement is contingent upon a child's continuing placement in substitute care.)

But Morris-Bilotti's concern goes beyond tinkering with the rules. The fundamental problem, she insists, is the virtual impossibility of empowering the poor—and lifting them permanently out of their poverty—"without disrupting a system whose very existence appears to be dependent upon maintaining the status quo."

The dilemma is real, particularly since social services constitute a significant aspect of the service industry, at a time more and more Americans must rely on the service sector for their livelihood. Social service workers, as Morris-Bilotti correctly concludes, can assure their own continued employment only by doing their work ineffectually.

"If we are to empower the consumer, it is our first and foremost responsibility to prepare him to live successfully without us."

(March 1991)

LOOKING FOR THE
REAL POTENTIAL

HERE'S THE WAY IT WORKS NOW: The state welfare agencies decide what services they will offer and to whom. Then applicants are screened to see which programs they qualify for. Is there a health problem? A child-abuse problem? A problem with housing, income, mental health? The caseworker will pick the appropriate program and...

We've done it that way so long that it almost seems the only way to do it.

But Sharon Morris-Bilotti has been toying with another approach that makes a lot more sense. Suppose, she says, that instead of looking for defects in "consumers" of welfare services (she thinks it demeaning to call them "clients" or "recipients"), we look for strengths. Suppose, that instead of devising programs to fix every personal shortcoming, we could focus on the barriers that keep people from fixing their own problems.

Morris-Bilotti has not devised such a system. In fact, the Illinois state welfare agency, for which she has worked for nearly 30 years, is organized pretty much along traditional lines. What she has done, to sometimes startlingly good effect, is to rethink her notions about welfare and to explore how we might do it better. For instance:

"If we want to build a system based on strengths, and are willing to sacrifice the convenience of our current deficit approach, we will have to reframe much of our thinking and most of our practice.... We would no longer see a child with Down's syndrome in terms of his developmental, cognitive and physical limitations; we would look instead at what he is ultimately capable of achieving."

Sure. But if you don't look for problems, how will you know what's needed?

"If we could forget about problems for a minute and concentrate on strengths and potential," says Morris-Bilotti, "we would be freed up to look for those factors that limit opportunities, to think about environmental enhancements that might lead to positive outcomes.... We can't change a person's inherent potential, so why not work on what we can do something about? Why not try to remove barriers to achievement and self-fulfillment?"

What she is talking about—her pipe dream, as she calls it—is a different kind of system: integrated at the local level, freed of categorical restrictions, and aimed at enhancing the well-being of individuals.

She describes a series of concentric circles: "The child with his or her full potential rests squarely in the middle; the family, as the child's most influential and immediate environment, surrounds the child. The next circle is the neighborhood and the larger community.... Each circle is concerned with the well-being and outcomes of those in the next circle in."

And how, in practical terms, might her pipe dream work? It could start, she suggests, with a survey to determine the actual status of children and families.

"This would, perhaps for the first time, provide mutually agreed upon, statewide human-services outcome goals, and it would provide a larger framework for the various agencies, with their vested interests, to respond to. It would also dictate an integrated, holistic approach that would encourage states to give priority to prevention and early intervention."

But goals would be set not just by states but also by local neighborhoods, which would be free to enlist businesses and other stakeholders in removing the barriers to family well-being. "They might define a barrier as something negative that exists, like illicit drug trafficking; or something positive that is missing, such as affordable child or elder care."

Morris-Bilotti's point is not to criticize social workers, who may be doing their enthusiastic best within a failed system, but to rethink the system. Like Chicago's John McKnight, she believes a better system would focus on potential, not deficits. Her emphasis would be on family-centered, community-based prevention, built around goals and evaluated by outcomes.

If that's a pipe dream, the rest of us had better find out what she's smoking.

(March 1991)

ON RACIAL MATTERS

WHEN RACISTS QUOTE ME

MY FRIEND DIDN'T DISAGREE with a recent column suggesting that black Americans—particularly the black middle class—must take primary responsibility for helping to lead the black underclass out of its poverty.

Indeed, he went out of his way to voice his agreement that it would be silly for the victims of racism to look to racists for their salvation. What bothered him, he said, was that racists reading the column could find in it support for their white-supremacist views.

"I no longer pay much attention," he said, "when [he named two blacks in the Reagan administration] say things that echo what the racists are saying. I've lost respect for them anyway. But when a respected person like yourself gives ammunition to the racists, then I guess my reaction is a little different. Doesn't it bother you that people will use what you say against the interest of black people?"

Well, of course it does. Does that mean I should stop saying what I believe to be true? I don't think so. Speaking the truth as you see it can create problems, no doubt. But the alternative strikes me as a good deal worse.

I first became aware of the problem years ago when I suggested that black Americans—or at any rate the black leadership—was expending too much time, energy and political capital in its push for busing, and far too little on improving education for black children.

That view, as far as I could ascertain, came very close to being the black American consensus. But it also served nicely the ends of those who thought racial integration was an abomination. I cringed when my columns were excerpted for editorials in opposition to school desegregation, or saw my words inserted by bigoted legislators into the *Congressional Record* in support of their views.

I took pains to put in enough qualifiers so that readers would understand that while I thought racial integration was a commendable goal, improved education for black children— wherever they attended school—was a better one. But there was no way I could keep editorialists or speakers or legislators from leaving out the qualifiers and reporting (accurately) that I thought we were spending too much time, money and energy on getting our children into white classrooms.

I finally stopped worrying about it. The only way to stop this unwelcome use of my words, I decided, was either to stop saying anything at all or else to stop saying anything with which the "enemy" might agree—even if, on a particular point, the "enemy" and I weren't that far apart.

I recall my first columns condemning Uganda's Idi Amin. I thought his administration was a murderous disgrace. So did most of the world, including most black Americans. But some friends thought I shouldn't say so because there were white bigots who would use my words to discredit black leadership generally.

And most particularly, I recall the long years when America's black leaders avoided any public statement implying that some of the problems facing blacks had to be solved by blacks themselves. Those same leaders would be candid enough when talking to black audiences, including their own friends and families. But for public consumption, the culprit was always racism, the solution always in the hands of white people. No fuel for the racists in that.

But not much help for racism's victims, either. One of the results of that blame-it-all-on-the-white-folks mentality is that it helped to produce a generation of children who saw themselves not as bright, capable youngsters with the ability to take control of their own destinies but as essentially helpless victims of a racism they could do nothing about.

It still bothers me that my words—perhaps including these— may provide fuel for people who do not have my interest at heart. But I believe that it is past time for us to start speaking with as much candor as we can muster about the problems that still confront us.

It is fair to say that racism is the source of many of those problems. But it is also fair to say that we have to take the lead in their solution: that there are some things we'll simply have to do for ourselves.

(July 1985)

BLACK AMERICA'S HOUSE

IS ON FIRE

ASK A HUNDRED BLACK AMERICANS what constitutes the biggest threat to their continued progress, and 90 of them are likely to answer: racism.

They will have no trouble coming up with evidence to support their view.

The controversy over Stanford University's official list of required great books, which includes no work by a black writer, suggests that even at the highest academic levels white Americans have trouble dealing fairly on racial issues.

The infamous remarks of Jimmy the Greek Snyder and Al Campanis, the continued display of the Confederate flag as a more-or-less official symbol in a number of southern states and the refusal of the federal government to elevate racism to the level of serious concern are evidence that racism, 1980s style, isn't necessarily subtle.

At the most blatant levels, it takes only a list of names to make the point: Bernhard Goetz, Howard Beach, Forsyth

County and Tawana Brawley, the black New York cheerleader who says she was gang-raped by six white men.

Racism still abounds in this country, though obviously to a lesser degree than formerly, and its effects still limit the opportunity and cripple the spirit of black Americans.

But for all that, it seems clear to me that racism is no longer the biggest threat to black America. That dubious honor lies much closer to home, in what is happening among blacks themselves.

Racism can be compared to the unfairness by which your grandfather cheated mine out of some of his property. That injustice demands to be redressed, the property lines redrawn.

But only a fool would stand at the fence screaming about property lines when his house is on fire.

Black America's house is on fire, and the evidence is plain to see:

- More than half of the black babies born in America are born out of wedlock, largely to adolescent mothers who lack the knowledge and the resources to get their youngsters off to a decent start in life.
- Illicit drugs sold by blacks to blacks are turning entire communities into disaster areas.
- Academic failure, including the deliberate rejection of academic exertion as unacceptably "white," is producing a generation of black Americans woefully unprepared for the increasingly technical demands of the work place.
- The leading cause of death among black youth is homicide, most of it involving blacks killing blacks.

It is not merely unfair to attribute this dismaying conflagration to racism; it is a distraction. We are obsessed with the search for racist arsonists when our time would be far better spent forming bucket brigades to douse the flames. There will be plenty of time to demand indemnity, if we still find that worthwhile, after the fire is out.

I do not doubt that racist sins, both of commission and of omission, are to blame for much of what is happening in our community. The lighted matches of overt discrimination and the oily rags of neglect have put the house in peril. But the urgent need now is to extinguish the flames.

A lot of us who understand that, and who understand further that the firefighting responsibility must be assumed by the occupants of the burning house, are reluctant to say so for fear that to do so is to let white people off the hook.

Imagine trying to combat the AIDS virus by focusing on its origins. We might be able to trace the first AIDS contamination in the United States to a Canadian airline steward. We might be able to show that AIDS first surfaced in East Africa (though the evidence for that is unreliable at best). But supposing we were able to trace the virus to the northeastern section of, say, Uganda, and to green monkeys of that region, and even to the particular green monkey that started the whole thing, what would we do with the culprit? Demand that it apologize? Would our tedious and successful search reduce by even one the number of deaths due to AIDS?

The reasonable course for dealing with effects of racism is the course we are taking with AIDS: to learn as much as we can about how to cure it, how to immunize ourselves against it and how to halt its tragic spread.

It is, in any case, a difficult undertaking, but I believe we have the wit to do it if we can bring ourselves to focus on doing it as our highest priority.

Sadly, we are more concerned with finding villains than with effecting cures. We are wasting our time, and precious lives, in a pointless search for green monkeys.

(February 1988)

A VISIT BY LOUIS FARRAKHAN

IT'S HARD TO KNOW which was more intriguing: watching Louis Farrakhan charm his way through a largely antagonistic interview or watching my colleagues—black, white and, especially, Jewish—react, regroup and reorganize their notions regarding this man.

The 2½-hour breakfast at the *Washington Post* Wednesday was the first time I'd seen the leader of the Nation of Islam in a situation where he could not count on standing ovations for even his most dubious statements. How would he handle the combination of genuine befuddlement and scarcely concealed hostility of the *Post*'s reporters, editors and executives? Would the entire morning be taken up with charges and denials of antisemitism? Would he claim misquotation and improper use of out-of-context snippets from his public utterances?

And would my colleagues evince any interest in his social and economic notions or in the Nation's manifest ability to transform the lives of black thugs and criminals?

He began disarmingly, with gratitude for the opportunity to exchange views with the newspaper's "esteemed writers and editors," then said:

"Louis Farrakhan is not an enemy of America, not an enemy of Jews, not an enemy of white people."

He said it with obvious sincerity, and yet it was equally obvious that many of those around the breakfast table left the meeting more convinced than ever of his anti-Jewish sentiments.

But if Jews at the table could see clear evidence of Farrakhan's almost naive antisemitism, blacks at the table could see with equal clarity one reason why he is able to attract and titillate black audiences in cities and on college campuses across America. It isn't that they buy the particulars of his economic ideas, or his notion of establishing an African-American nation on the African continent.

Farrakhan says what so many black people believe but have learned not to say in public: for instance, that Jews wield tremendous influence in the news and entertainment media. That doesn't mean that most blacks accept Farrakhan's notion of a small Jewish cabal that meets in Hollywood or in a Park Avenue apartment to decide which ideas and trends are to be foisted off on the public. But few of us doubt the disproportionate influence of Jews—for good or ill—on what we see on television or in the movies.

Nor do blacks doubt the disproportionate influence of Jews on American foreign policy, particularly with regard to political and economic support of Israel.

But we also know that to say these things is to be accused of antisemitism. That's why blacks can cheer when Farrakhan says them, even in gross overstatement.

And he does overstate, frequently painting Jews as particularly responsible for the villainy of white America generally: the slave trade, for instance, or the hypocritical practice of religion.

Farrakhan has the demagogue's facility for giving people a scapegoat for their frustrations. To blacks bumping the glass ceiling of career progress, or frightened by the growth of the black underclass and the slaughter of young black men, or torn by self-doubt, he offers a white—and Jewish—conspiracy.

And the suspicion is that he knows what he is doing. Give him 15 minutes and he can explain that he meant no anti-Jewish animosity when he referred to Judaism as a "dirty religion," or described Hitler as "wickedly great," or that his sweeping criticism of Jews is not different from his occasional criticism of specific black leaders. But he has to know that these gratuitous references will be interpreted as antisemitism. Perhaps he really is more antisemitic than he imagines; perhaps he is simply more concerned with the adulation of blacks than with the sensitivity of Jews.

But even for blacks, what he offers is far closer to exoneration (drug murders as evidence of genocide rather than of inner-city lawlessness, for instance) than to a specific plan for economic salvation.

Two areas in which the Nation of Islam has recorded extraordinary success are the reclamation of drug-infested neighborhoods and the rehabilitation of black criminals. Some of us wanted to know how the Nation does it, whether the rehabilitative success can be spread from the prisons to the black schools and communities, and the extent to which the inculcation of black pride can be separated from the specifics of religion.

We wanted to hear him explain why he has been unable to translate black admiration for his oratory into widespread support for his economics.

But the preoccupation with antisemitism carried the day—we allowed it to carry the day, in part because we wanted to be sensitive to our colleagues to whom it seemed to matter so much; partly because the dialogue was, for a time, entertaining. At the end, however, we were left to wonder how much substance and depth there is to this bold, charming and, yes, disturbing man.

(March 1990)

PLAYING ON WHITE GUILT

THE LATE MARCUS STEWART, my first newspaper boss, was an embarrassment to some of us younger members of his staff. He was a canny publisher, an astute observer of the human condition and a fine newspaperman. We knew that.

What embarrassed us was the condition of the offices of the black-oriented *Indianapolis Recorder*: disheveled and cheerless, bare bulbs dangling from the ceiling, tin patches covering worn-out sections of the floor. When a couple of us finally got up the nerve to suggest that the paper might gain a little self-respect for itself if he fixed the place up, his response was something like this:

White advertisers aren't going to give you any business if they think you're doing too well. What is more important: a new floor, or the revenues that keep the roof over our heads?

He had weighed the options for a generation, and he had made peace with his conclusion: you don't put on your best suit to go begging.

Two things about Mark Stewart. First, for a variety of reasons (including the discovery that "charitable" advertising was no longer enough to keep the business afloat and that, at the end, he had to persuade his advertisers that he could deliver for them a market they coveted) he finally abandoned the old *Recorder* building and bought a nifty new building on the other side of town. Second, a lot of people who today would sneer at his erstwhile poor-mouthing are in fact repeating his tactic.

They paint our condition—the condition of black America—in inappropriately drab colors, not merely insisting on pointing out the economic, social and political gap between us and white America but also going out of their way to deny any contention that, for some of us at least, things might be getting better.

Like my old boss, they believe that accentuating the negative is the best chance of winning concessions from white folk. Not for them the approach that says: "Look how much we have done with so little; doesn't that prove that all we need is greater opportunity?" No, their appeal is less to justice than to pity. You don't put on your best suit to go begging.

And it is begging, whether it is done humbly, on your knees, or militantly, with your fist thrust in the air.

Look at the gaps, we say. The academic achievement gap, the college attendance gap, the income gap—can't you see how pitiful we are and how much in need of special consideration? And if one of the gaps shows signs of closing, we simply accentuate another. For instance, the evidence in recent years that the income of two-earner black households has reached 85 percent of parity and that the remaining gap is closing at the rate of 5 percent a year, elicits no cheers. It only prompts a new focus on the growing income gap for single-income black families.

There would be nothing wrong with stressing that alternative truth if the idea was to trigger a shift in priorities—from more concessions for well-off blacks to the crying needs of single-parent black households. The purpose, however, is not to change priorities but to drive home the idea that black America generally is still doing badly and is still in need of concessions.

Thus the plight of the black underclass is highlighted, not in the name of doing something about the underclass, but to extract concessions for the black middle class. The joblessness, hopelessness and despair of the ghettos are used as the basis for affirmative-action promotions for the black middle class and special college admissions for their children.

It is like demanding that the society supply aspirin for your uncle because your nephew has a headache. Isn't it time to abandon this bait-and-switch game in favor of truth in labeling?

What would come of such honesty? What would happen if we rearranged our priorities and not merely our rhetoric? We might fashion set-aside programs calculated to create job opportunities for the jobless and the underemployed rather than opportunities for a handful of well-connected minority entrepreneurs. We might propose schemes for enhancing college-going opportunities for the poor rather than special-admissions for the sons and daughters of well-off blacks. We might look for ways to encourage today's poor along the paths that led an earlier generation out of poverty. In short, we might look for ways to help the poor instead of merely using the poor for our own middle-class advantage.

It hardly need be said that even for the best-off blacks, racial disadvantage remains a bitter fact of life. Few of us are so naive as to suppose that even the best-prepared blacks are reaping the full benefits of their preparation or that they have some-how managed to overcome the continuing effects of racism.

But while racism and disadvantage may affect us all, it does not affect us all equally. Doesn't it make sense, particularly during this period when both resources and sympathy are in short supply, to sort out our priorities, to demand special help for those most in need of it?

So why don't we do it? The answer, I am convinced, is that we see advantage for ourselves in appeals to white guilt, and we fear that to acknowledge the very real progress that some of us have made is to reduce the guilt.

You don't put on your best suit to go begging.

(May 1990)

WHEN PUSH COMES TO SHOVE

THERE ARE SERIOUS ISSUES in the fight between Nike, Inc., and Operation PUSH, and there is also some hocus-pocus.

The serious issues include whether the company is taking advantage of black inner-city youngsters (who favor Nike's high-priced athletic shoes) and doing too little for the black community. Nike, pointing to its charitable contributions, its affirmative-action hiring practices and its use of black heroes in its television ads, says it is doing a lot and intends to do a lot more. PUSH, stressing Nike's black-generated profits, its dearth of blacks in top management and its reluctance to negotiate the questions, says the company deserves to be boycotted by blacks.

Here's the hocus-pocus: the basis for PUSH's demands is the "exploitation" of inner-city youngsters; poor families are spending $100 a pair and more for Nike's athletic shoes, when their meager resources ought to be spent on more important things. The proposed solution is to place more blacks in top

management positions, including seats on the board of direc-
tors, and buy more advertising from black-owned media outlets.

But if poor black kids are the "victims" of Nike's sales
success, how are they helped by helping a handful of black
executives to get better jobs? If low-income black families are
being exploited by Nike's aggressive marketing, how is that
exploitation reduced by forcing the company to advertise in
black outlets, which presumably would expose yet more black
youngsters to the lure of the shoes?

Like so many of the affirmative-action proposals, it amounts
to a bait-and-switch game. The inner-city poor furnish the
statistical base for the proposals, but the benefits go primarily
to the already well-off.

The tactic is to use the plight of poor blacks to prove that
blacks in the aggregate are underrepresented in college, graduate school or top management. The result is that some blacks—
most likely those that have been least crippled by racism—get
special-admission college seats and affirmative-action promotions.

My children—and the children of my middle-class colleagues,
who already enjoy important advantages—no longer need to
compete with their white counterparts. They compete instead
with the children of Anacostia, Watts, Hough, Cabrini Green
and Overtown—a competition they are likely to win. Black
executives who already hold good jobs get promoted to better
ones; blacks who already sit on important corporate boards get
another directorship. And the people who provide the statistical base get nothing.

The point is not to absolve Nike (or any other company) of
its corporate-citizenship responsibilities but to show the hocus-
pocus of giving further advantage to the already advantaged in
the name of doing something for the poor.

The truth is, I don't know whether Nike is doing less for
black America than its rival Reebok, which allegedly has
escaped the boycotters' wrath by giving money to PUSH.
Arguably, it should be doing a lot more.

Furthermore PUSH has a point when it argues that
Georgetown basketball coach John Thompson, who earns

some $200,000 a year in Nike endorsements, and basketball star Michael Jordan may be in good position to comment on the quality of Nike's shoes but, having no corporate responsibility, are in no position to comment on Nike's corporate behavior.

"We're simply using our legitimate consumer right not to do business with companies that do not do business with us," said Tyrone Crider, successor to PUSH founder Jesse Jackson as executive director of the Chicago-based organization.

No argument there, though it is worth noting that there is a distinction between a consumer boycott and extortion—between demands that the company do more for its customers and demands that it do more for PUSH.

I'd feel better about the PUSH effort if its demands included scholarships for inner-city children or gym equipment for inner-city neighborhoods or anything else to ameliorate the "exploitation" of the poor.

I know too much about the "glass ceiling" that limits the aspirations of female and minority managers to argue that Nike and the rest of corporate America have done all they should to break the hegemony of white males. We are a long way from parity in the executive suites and the boardrooms, and there's nothing wrong with demanding more.

My problem is the hocus-pocus of using the plight of the black poor to further those demands. The fact is we are talking about two different sets of problems: discrimination against middle-class black executives, on the one hand, and the thoroughgoing disadvantage of the black poor, on the other. Both need to be addressed, but it is dishonest to pretend that applying a tourniquet to the well-off will stop the bleeding of the poor.

What does it do for the poor for Nike to hire an upper-middle-class black executive from another company to be a vice president at Nike, or to give Vernon Jordan another seat on a corporate board?

(August 1990)

CELEBRATING VICTIMIZATION

ASK A HUNDRED BLACK AMERICANS about the state of race relations in the country, and maybe 90 will tell you things are getting worse. On the job, in the general society, on the most prestigious college campuses, you will hear talk—and chapter-and-verse examples—of growing resurgent racism: ignorant insensitivity, racial slights, open bigotry.

Can the country that has seen blacks achieve leadership in industry and in the professions—that has moved so far beyond the question of voting rights that Mississippi has elected a black member of Congress and Virginia a governor—also be a place where racism grows worse with each passing year?

Julius Lester, the 1960s radical who authored *Look Out, Whitey! Black Power's Gon' Get Your Mama*, offers an intriguing explanation of the seeming paradox: Black Americans, having achieved the "possible" dream of securing civil rights, are now embarked on a "disastrously divisive and impossible" task of fighting racism.

"The first thing to understand about the civil rights movement," says Lester, now a professor of Jewish studies at the University of Massachusetts, "is that it won. It had set out in the mid-'50s to change the apartheid system of racial segregation in public places. With the passage of the 1964 Civil Rights Act, that was accomplished. In the early '60s, the movement set out to ensure that blacks had access to the voting booth. With the passage of the 1965 Voting Rights Act, that was accomplished. Much still needed to be done to implement and enforce those acts, but the legal principles of 'freedom and justice for all' had been reiterated and given a new formulation in law."

But then something remarkable—but largely unremarked—happened. The civil rights movement shifted its focus to something called "human rights"—a quest not for constitutional guarantees but for changed attitudes. The new focus "said, in effect, that the opinions, feelings, and prejudices of private individuals was a legitimate target of political action," a reorientation that Lester finds not merely inappropriate—"a new statement of totalitarianism"—but dangerous.

"The shift from fighting for civil rights to fighting against racism," Lester told a recent audience of the National Forum Foundation, "was a shift from seeking and finding common ground to a position that has been disastrously divisive. To fight against racism divides humanity into us against them. It leads to a self-definition as 'victim,' and anyone who defines himself as a victim has found a way to keep himself in a perpetual state of self-righteous self-pity and anger. And that, in a nutshell, is the state of black America today."

Lester's words, which went down easily at the largely conservative forum, will be hard for most blacks to swallow. Has this former revolutionary become so content with his lofty academic position that he cannot see the racism that abounds in America? Does he counsel black Americans to take no notice of the thoroughgoing racism that is a fact of their daily lives?

Not quite. His point is not to deny the existence of racism but to point out the inherently divisive effect of focusing on it, at least in terms of privately held prejudices.

"Racism is an issue in the public domain to the extent that it violates my rights as a citizen," he said. "And the society is still in the midst of trying to determine how we ascertain when that has occurred. This is much of what lies at the center of the debates on affirmative action." But there is no "right not to be bothered by racism. It would be nice. It is certainly desirable. But the fact remains, there is no *right* to be free from racism, antisemitism or sexism."

And yet it is the very attempt to force the eradication of "isms" from American life that may account for the racial strife on college campuses and elsewhere. What to black students seems a reasonable demand—that their campuses be free of racist attitudes—may look to white students as demands for special privilege, special accommodations and special curricula. As San Jose State's Shelby Steele has observed, there is political power in proving that you are the victim of racist attitudes. Much of the political clout that black students on predominantly white campuses are able to wield comes from painting themselves as victims.

But in order to sustain itself, that power requires that the victims go on celebrating their victimization, and it encourages other groups—women, ethnics, gays, even heterosexual white males—to establish themselves as victims as a means to countervailing political power. The result is to undermine the sense of community on campus.

Lester sees it as one of the critical differences between today's racial activism and that of the '50s and '60s.

"The impression is given today that the civil rights movement was a black movement. It was not. It was an integrated movement, and innumerable whites also risked their lives and sanity for the principle of 'freedom and justice for all.' It is startling to remember the integrated nature of the movement, its self-conscious and un-self-conscious reaching across cultural and class differences to learn from and with each other. It is startling to remember that period and look at today, when blacks and whites are more separated than ever and the only bridge the two have to each other is a mutual animosity."

The civil rights movement was a search for community, and its appeal was to commonality. Today's movement is a search for proof of victimization, and its appeal is to difference. And maybe that's why things seem so much worse than they used to be.

(May 1990)

HE'S A RACIST—THE EASY ANSWER

THE YOUNGSTERS, ALL BLACK COLLEGIANS, were discussing the relative merits of historically black versus predominantly white colleges, but one of them said something that I think has wider implications than any of us recognized at the time:

"One of the big advantages of going to a black school is that you have four years of not hassling about race. I know it's not the real world, and sooner or later you have to deal with the race issue, but it's nice to have a period in your life when you don't have to think about it all the time."

When I urged her to say more, she said something that has been on my mind ever since:

"Say there's a professor, or maybe another student, who doesn't like you. You may not know the reason, but at a black school, with black instructors and black classmates, you know it's not because you're black, so you do a personality check. Do I come on too strong? Am I argumentative? Does he think I'm trying to get by on b.s. rather than studying the material he assigned? Am I acting like a snob?

"Maybe he's just a creep, and it's not your fault at all. But the point is, with a black professor or classmate, you ask yourself the questions. If he's white, you'll probably just decide he's racist, and that's the end of it."

The point, which may illuminate much of the racial angst that so occupies us these days, is this: If race is a possible explanation for a negative comment or attitude, there's a strong temptation to conclude that it *is* the explanation. No introspection, no self-examination, no "personality check"—and no opportunity for personal growth.

Black people used to joke about the applicant for a radio announcer's job who complained that he wasn't hired "b-b-b-because I'm b-b-black." I haven't heard the joke in recent years—not, I suspect, because it's old but because it's no longer funny. We are too sure that any slight we suffer at the hands of whites is because we're black.

Racism has become our all-purpose explanation for every disadvantage. Racist editors "mess with" our copy. Racist bar examiners learn to spot "black" writing in anonymous bar exam papers and give the writer undeservedly bad marks. Racist policy makers depreciate our wisdom and insights. Racist personnel officers discount our résumés and interviews.

And in every case, the possibility exists that we are right. I talked recently with a friend who applied, along with a handful of whites, for a job as a congressional aide. He was the only one who was asked to take a written examination.

Had he run into a racist interviewer who was looking for a good reason to turn him down? Quite likely. After all, he didn't get the job. But it is also possible that my friend— experienced and bright—was being considered for a more responsible position than the one for which he had applied. And it is at least conceivable that (1) his test results are still being evaluated or (2) that his ill-concealed outrage at being singled out for testing made him appear "uncooperative" or "uncollegial."

I don't think he misread what was happening to him. But he *might* have; and if he did, he might have cost himself a good job.

That's the eternal risk of the automatic race-based explanation. The white professor who just might be trying to fan a spark of brilliance; the white personnel officer who just might be wondering if he has discovered a diamond in the rough; the white interviewer who just might be looking for a basis to turn a negative impression into a more positive one; the white judge who just may be trying to nudge a lawyer toward a more productive line of questioning but, if met with resistance and resentment, decides he's talking to a guy with a chip on his shoulder and the hell with him.

But even if the initial suspicions are correct, what is to be lost by giving the benefit of the doubt? At least occasionally, an innocent response—the "soft answer [that] turneth away wrath"—might prompt a racist to embarrassment, to the advantage of his intended victim. The response that says "We both know you're a racist" merely seals the disadvantage.

What I am about to say will sound like heresy to many—probably most—blacks. But I think reliance on race as the universal explainer does more harm than good. It inhibits our achievement by limiting our ability to try. It oversimplifies complex interpersonal relations and reduces our own role in their improvement.

It even mars our successes. Ask a well-placed black professional if he thinks he got his job because he is good or because he is black, and you'll be surprised how often the answer comes back: "Because I'm black." (A white person who even suggests that the black professional was hired because of his race is, of course, a racist.)

I can't say too clearly that the racial explanation may often be the correct one. But it is, in my view, frequently a damaging one. People who are successful are most often those who believe themselves to be in control of their own fate. The race-is-all explanation gives that control to others. It says that we are limited not by the things that we can control—hard work, study, self-analysis—but by two things that are clearly beyond our ability to change: our black skins and white racists.

(July 1990)

MINORITIES INTO THE
MAINSTREAM

A COALITION OF THE NATION'S top business and academic
leaders has called for a new national effort—comparable to the
civil rights movement of a generation ago—to help boost
minorities into the American mainstream.

The report of the Business-Higher Education Forum, osten-
sibly representing the views of more than 90 university and
Fortune 500 CEOs, is remarkably focused, serious and candid.
The candor begins with the title of the 87-page report released
here Wednesday: "Three Realities: Minority Life in the United
States."

The first reality is that a lot of minority group members are
"making it" by any economic, social or cultural yardstick.

"A growing middle class—black and Hispanic—is repeating
the previous successes of ethnic immigrants and is doing it in
much the same way: by insisting that they be treated with the
dignity to which every human being is entitled; by demanding
the equal treatment that is every citizen's due; and by dili-

gence, education, seizing each new opportunity, and sacrificing today for the tomorrow of their children."

The second reality is the situation of minorities at the margin: the working poor whose undereducation and lack of marketable skills "prevent them from keeping pace with the rising demands of the workplace—despite their best efforts."

The third reality comprises the poor and the underclass, whose plight is unchanged and whose numbers are growing.

The three realities describe what we already know but have been strangely unwilling to talk about. Perhaps our minority leadership, which came of age during the civil rights movement and which still uses the civil rights appellation to describe itself, is locked in the memory of the days when (at least in the South) class and attitudinal differences within the group were largely irrelevant. Perhaps it is the fear that acknowledging the palpable progress of at least some blacks and Hispanics might let whites "off the hook," leading them to ascribe the plight of the marginal and the poor to their own personal shortcomings.

Whatever the reason, the theme of the racial advocates— blacks in particular—has been that we are all equally victimized by racism. And one result is that the remedies they propose (affirmative action, set-asides, special admissions) frequently serve the interests of the least badly off.

"Three Realities" recognizes that, though the three groups do suffer some of the same indignities, their different circumstances dictate different remedies and different priorities, with the hardest-hit groups at the top of the list.

The recommendations are directed at three different areas:

Public Policy. The report calls for full teenage employment by the year 2000; inflation-indexing of public employment and training programs to their 1980 budget levels; a redesign of public assistance to avoid discouraging work and education; programs to discourage teenage pregnancy and leaving school; full funding of Head Start and Chapter I programs, and the restructuring of student-assistance programs so parents can know by the time their children are in seventh grade that "given high enough achievement, their college education costs will be guaranteed."

Colleges and Universities. Such strategies as "prep years" on campus, tutorial and mentoring programs and departmental recruitment goals should be undertaken to increase the enrollment and graduation rates of minorities. Moreover, affirmative action should be expanded to cover the nonacademic aspects of colleges and universities, including job training, contracting with minority firms and otherwise "making the most of the institutions' considerable presence in their communities as business entities."

Corporations. The recommendations include expansion of entry-level and middle-management job opportunities for minorities, family-oriented policies including child care, capital development schemes and finding ways to increase minority opportunities in franchising.

The task force that produced the report (cochairs: Clifton Wharton, Jr., chairman and CEO of the nation's largest pension fund, and Steven C. Mason, president and chief operating officer of the Mead Corp.) makes clear the changed nature of the racial struggle and the need for new strategies.

"A generation ago, a cadre of determined, able, and dedicated men and women threw themselves into the civil rights struggle because they understood that achieving political rights was of paramount importance. That phase of the battle has, by and large, been won.

"But now an unfinished cause issues its call: the struggle for economic equality for minorities. Victory in this struggle is by no means assured. If it is to be attained, it will require new sacrifices, new energies and a new version of the practical vision that has already made good on the promise of political equality."

It will also require what may be the key missing ingredient: a sense of urgency.

(June 1990)

No Conspiracy

D.C. MAYOR MARION BARRY has been tried, convicted and sentenced for cocaine possession. He has acknowledged using cocaine over some period of time. He describes himself as a recovering drug abuser.

And yet there are among his supporters those who will tell you—who earnestly believe—that Barry is a victim not of his own bad choices but of a nationwide conspiracy against black politicians.

Indeed, that "they" are out to discredit black elected officials is among the milder charges of the conspiracy-minded. The serious conspiratorialists are convinced that white America—specifically including the national government—is embarked on a scheme to do in blacks generally, a program of black genocide.

The *New York Times* recently published the results of a telephone survey of 1,000 New Yorkers on three often-cited elements of the anti-black conspiracy: that the government deliberately singles out and investigates black elected officials in order to discredit them; that the government deliberately sees to it that illicit drugs are available in low-income black neighborhoods; and that the AIDS virus was deliberately created to infect and destroy black people.

The findings: Three out of four black New Yorkers believe that it is true, or at least *possibly* true, that black politicians have been targeted by the government; 60 percent of blacks believe that it is true, or may be true, that the government is part of a conspiracy to put drugs into black neighborhoods; and 29 percent of blacks credit the notion that AIDS has been engineered to destroy blacks. (Whites believe that the charges are "almost certainly not true" by margins ranging from 57 percent in the case of black politicians, to 75 percent on the question of drugs, to 91 percent for AIDS.)

The biggest surprise for me was the finding that 63 percent of black New Yorkers think it is "almost certainly not true" that the AIDS virus was deliberately created to destroy blacks. (It's too bad the *Times* and WCBS-TV, which jointly conducted the poll, didn't ask whether AIDS was a deliberate attempt to wipe out homosexuals; the "almost certainly not true" category might have been dramatically smaller.)

I am not at all surprised at the other answers. As a matter of fact, if the question of conspiracy had been put more broadly, I might have joined the "might possibly be true" crowd. While I do not believe that there is any conspiracy in the sense of an orchestrated plan by the government to remove black officials from office, I would not be surprised to learn that at least some of the decisions to investigate public officials are politically— and by extension, racially—motivated. I have in mind cases ranging from J. Edgar Hoover's dogged campaign against Martin Luther King, Jr., to the present administration's apparently abortive effort to nail Rep. William Gray (D-Pa.)

Ask me whether I believe the government's anti-drug effort might be more aggressively pursued if the primary victims of the drug traffic were young whites, and again I'd admit the possibility. Indeed, if you define "conspiracy" to include not just a coordinated plan of action but also widely held negative attitudes, I'd say there is at the very least a conspiracy of neglect against the black poor.

But that isn't what the *New York Times*/WCBS-TV respondents seem to have had in mind. Their belief is in a government plot to embarrass, displace or destroy blacks, by means of selective investigations and prosecutions, enticement to drug abuse and spread of AIDS. And I find much of that sort of thinking to be little more than a desire to escape personal responsibility.

Black Washingtonians, for instance, may believe (as I do) that the government went to unacceptable lengths to lure Barry into a situation where he could be videotaped using crack cocaine. But we must also believe that the decision to use crack—during the FBI sting and before—was Barry's own. It may be that the government would move with greater alacrity to combat drug trafficking if its victims included thousands of white youngsters, but it doesn't follow that the deaths of black youngsters are a calculated objective of the government or that the inner-city neighborhoods where drugs take their tragic toll have no responsibility for allowing the traffic to continue.

The trouble with laying the problems of black America at the feet of white conspirators is that it frustrates the search for solutions.

Define the troubles of black officials in terms of conspiracy, and blacks find themselves coming to the defense of people they ought to be kicking out of office. Define drug abuse or AIDS among blacks as products of a white conspiracy, and blacks are likely to spend more time proving the conspiracy than doing what they can to save black lives.

Whites may do less than they could, because they care less than they should, about the problems facing black America. But that doesn't absolve black America of the need to spend more effort addressing those problems and less in a fruitless search for scapegoats.

(October 1990)

CONSPIRACY AGAINST BLACKS?

SURE, WHY NOT?

THERE AREN'T MANY THINGS you can count on in these uncertain times, but there is one. Let me make a speech before a black audience and sometime during the Q&A someone is certain to ask if I believe there is a conspiracy against black Americans.

It doesn't matter whether the subject is drugs or joblessness, school failure or teen pregnancy, politics or immigration. I can count on hearing some version of the conspiracy question. My habit has been to answer no. Sometimes I take the approach that one shouldn't embrace complicated explanations when simpler ones suffice. Sometimes I point out that many of the terrible things that happen to us are the unintended consequences of our own misguided policy proposals. And sometimes I resort to humor.

"I've worked intimately with white people for most of my life," I'll say. "And the one thing of which I'm absolutely certain is that they aren't smart enough to sustain a conspiracy of the scope and complexity necessary to account for all our troubles."

I'm starting to think that maybe I've been giving the wrong answer. No, I haven't come across compelling new evidence of a gigantic conspiracy. It simply occurs to me that making black Americans believe that such a conspiracy exists may be the best thing that could happen to us.

I've heard well-educated professionals argue, for instance, that the drug traffic and its concomitant homicides are a part of a conspiracy to eliminate black men. White people import the drugs, white bankers launder the drug money, and white people garner most of the profits (both from the drug sales and from the gold chains, leather coats and fancy cars preferred by drug dealers). White people even import and sell the AK-47s and the Uzis that black drug dealers use to slaughter each other. Ergo: the slaughter of black men is a white conspiracy, and drugs are the tool these clever devils have chosen to carry out their plan.

It doesn't make sense to me, but no matter. I think I'll start agreeing. Just the other day, the *Post* had a story of a young woman who smoked "three five-dollar rocks" of crack cocaine to ease her labor pains—knowing that her baby might be born brain-damaged as a result. Suppose someone had been able to convince her of a white conspiracy to produce brain-damaged black babies. Isn't there a chance that she might have made up her mind to seek drug treatment rather than play into the hands of racists?

If our young men could be made to see their gold chains and gold-rimmed BMWs as evidence of their complicity in a white-run conspiracy, might they not be embarrassed into getting out of the drug business (or else driven out of it by their enraged peers)?

Even Rayful Edmond, the recently convicted "kingpin" of Washington drug traffickers, might have turned his considerable entrepreneurial skills to legitimate business if he had come to see himself as an unwitting dupe in a white-run scheme to wipe out young black men.

The possibilities are endless. Convince youngsters in the black inner cities that their undereducation is the result of a white conspiracy, and maybe they'd abandon their notion that studying hard and speaking well amounts to "acting white." "Hey, white folks want me to stay dumb and stupid," they might say. "You think I'm going to be a chump and play into their hands?"

Convince our children that racist whites want them to have babies before they are mature enough to take care of them (and also to avoid both marriage and prenatal care) because it is to white folks' advantage that our children either die or live in poverty, and maybe our children will take a new look at their options.

Nor is it just the children who would benefit from the conspiracy idea. Suppose black people could be made to believe that conspiracy-minded whites have decided to undermine our economic viability by keeping us in the role of consumers and marginal employees. Might we not rise up in righteous indignation and go into business for ourselves, or at least support the businesses of our fellow blacks? Wouldn't we tell our children of the conspiracy and encourage them to think business?

Wouldn't some of our people take even low-paying jobs if we could persuade them that white conspirators wanted to control us by keeping us on welfare? We might even learn to eschew junk food, designer clothes and nonproductive spending if we were persuaded that these habits had been foisted off on us by whites scheming to keep us economically marginal.

The more I think of it, the more I'm convinced that spreading the word (however false) of a white conspiracy may be the best way to force us to tackle the whole range of problems confronting black America.

Is there a white conspiracy? The trouble is not with the illogic of the question. The trouble is our refusal to behave as though we believe the answer is yes.

(December 1989)

BLACK CREATIVITY,

BLACK SOLUTIONS

BLACK AMERICA HAS PROBLEMS: educational problems, employment problems, crime problems, drug problems; problems with family disintegration, neighborhood disorganization and racial disadvantage of all sorts.

Indeed, it sometimes seems to me that we cherish our problems.

Our journalists make a living writing about them. Our politicians get elected to office on the strength of them. Our scholars use our problems as the easiest route to social-policy influence. Our civil rights organizations rely on the "ownership" of our problems as a way of perpetuating their influence.

Indeed, a stranger to America might be forgiven for imagining that we see our problems as a sort of negative asset.

Well, it occurs to me that we have at least two important positive assets—brains and money—that might be combined to launch an attack on the problems that beset us.

What I have in mind is this: instead of endlessly talking

about our problems in a futile attempt to create societal guilt, I'd like to see our civil rights leadership turn its attention to imaginative solutions—tapping not only the intellectual capabilities of those who can map strategic assaults on the problems that beset us but also the mother wit of those unsung heroes and heroines who, on a daily basis, contribute their bit to making life better for those left behind.

The present tendency, largely unarticulated, is to assume that white people—the government and the society at large—know what needs to be done and that their failure to do it is simply evidence that we have failed to make them understand the extent of their racist guilt.

At some levels, that may be true. The "glass ceiling" that frustrates the ambition of so many well-qualified black executives, the routine discounting of the wisdom and insights of black workers, the inability of white managers to see leadership potential in black staffers—all these problems can be reduced by increasing white sensitivity.

But when it comes to our most pressing problems—teen pregnancy, crime, academic indifference, the dearth of role models, advocates and mentors, the shortsightedness that keeps so many of our youngsters from seeing the opportunities that do exist for them—the initiative has to be ours. We must devise, test and replicate the programs to inspire them, build their pride and self-esteem and give them the confidence to believe they can make it.

And I think we have to do these things before we can expect much financial help from a society that is reluctant to spend more of its shrinking resources on programs whose efficacy is in doubt.

But even the best-designed programs need financing. That's where our second positive asset comes in. Black Americans still lag far behind whites in income and wealth, but some of us are doing very well. Many black athletes and entertainers earn truly stupendous amounts of money, though too few of them are identified with programs designed to make things better for the masses of blacks. The reason, I suspect, is not selfishness but the dearth of programs of demonstrated effectiveness.

If our leadership can come up with effective approaches, couldn't we call upon our well-paid heroes to fund a series of pilot programs to show the wider society what can be done?

I recognize that some of our top earners already have given generously—not just Bill Cosby, with his $20 million gift to Spelman College, and Oprah Winfrey, whose contributions are regularly noted, but others who give both time and money to enterprises of all sorts. I also imagine that a lot of people—the Magic Johnsons and Michael Jordans, the Ray Leonards and Mike Tysons, the Michael Jacksons and the Eddie Murphys— may be doing a lot of giving that never makes the headlines.

But I believe these athletes and entertainers could be talked into launching a major funding source for black businesses, institutions or self-help projects certified by the civil rights leadership as worthwhile.

And not just these famous dozens, but also the thousands of actors, producers, physicians, lawyers, entrepreneurs and pro- fessionals who would respond to an appeal to do something for the masses of blacks.

Some of the projects thus funded would fail. Others would have to be rethought. But it seems beyond doubt that many of them would become so successful that they would commend themselves for adoption—and long-term funding—by the government.

What is missing is a vehicle for creating the necessary programs, a respected body of leaders to certify them as worthwhile, and the will to shift our attention from celebrat- ing our problems to solving them.

We've got the brains, and we've got the money. Can we also, at the risk of seeming to let white people off the hook, also summon up the will to save ourselves?

There are probably a thousand reasons why this simple idea won't work, and maybe even a dozen reasons why it shouldn't. But is there really any good reason not to try?

(March 1990)

THE CURE IS IN BLACK AMERICA

YOU CAN THINK of Glenn C. Loury (accurately) as one of the new breed of "black conservatives"—out of step with the mainstream black leadership and insufficiently critical of the Reagan administration—and dismiss him out of hand.

Or you can listen to this Harvard professor of political economy, judging his analysis of the problems confronting the black "underclass" and his prescriptions for change by the yardstick of common sense.

Perhaps because his views, in the current issue of *The Public Interest*, sound so much like what I have been trying to say, I prefer to listen to him when he says that much of the cure for what ails black America must be provided by black America itself.

He begins with a statement of the opposite point of view: that the problems that beset the black underclass, including family instability and crime, "are themselves manifestations of oppression—the historical and ongoing racism of the 'enemy without'—and that to focus on self-help strategies aimed at the behavior of blacks is to treat the symptoms of oppression, not its causes.

"If jobs were provided for those seeking work [still making the counter-argument], and if a commitment to civil rights could be restored at top levels of government, these internal problems would surely take care of themselves."

But: "I believe this argument to be seriously mistaken, and under certain circumstances possibly quite dangerous, for it invariably ends by placing the responsibility for the maintenance of personal values and social norms among poor blacks on the shoulders of those who do not have an abiding interest in such matters."

Loury is trying, in short, to distinguish between "fault" (the link between racism and the pathology of the ghetto) and "responsibility" (the question of who must take the lead in resolving the problems).

It may be fair to assign the fault to racist whites, he argues, but the responsibility rests on blacks, because "no people can be genuinely free so long as they look to others for their deliverance."

To some degree, Loury is pummeling a horse that is, if not dead, at least on its death bed. Most of the black leadership has begun to accept the notion that the next steps in the march toward equality must be choreographed and directed by blacks themselves. The question is not so much who should do it as what to do. Loury offers a suggestion:

"The next frontier for the [civil rights] movement should be a concerted effort to grapple directly with the difficult, internal problems which lower-class blacks now face.... To the extent that we can foster institutions within the black community that encourage responsible male involvement in parenting, help prevent unplanned pregnancies and support young unwed mothers in their efforts to return to school and become self-supporting, important changes in the lives of the most vulnerable segment of the black population can be made."

Loury is talking, quite unabashedly, about the necessity of

changing the behavior of the black underclass—something the black leadership (until quite recently) has been reluctant to discuss for fear of lending support to the claim of bigots that blacks are somehow unworthy and inferior.

But, says Loury, it is beyond debate that the "values, social norms and personal behaviors often observed among the poorest members of the black community are quite distinct from those characteristic of the black middle class." This "growing divergence," if unaddressed, will make it virtually impossible for the poorest of blacks to improve their circumstances—even "with the return of economic prosperity, with the election of a liberal Democrat to the presidency, or with the doubling in size of the Congressional Black Caucus."

The fundamental requirement for change, says Loury, is a revitalized and intensified moral leadership. And that is something that only blacks themselves can provide.

(July 1986)

BLACKS NEED PROGRAMS,
NOT BROMIDES

ANYBODY WHO CAN LOOK YOU IN THE EYE and tell you black America is in good shape and getting better is either a fraud or a fool. John E. Jacob, president of the National Urban League, is neither, and his pessimism at yesterday's 15th annual "State of Black America" press conference was hardly surprising.

Still it is becoming harder and harder to take these affairs seriously: not because the diagnoses are wrong but because the prescriptions are vague to the point of incoherence.

America must reorder its priorities, end its racism, invest in its "human capital," intensify its commitment to educate minorities, meet the unmet needs of all its people, undertake a "domestic Marshall Plan." You know the drill, and you know also that the exhortations are empty of the sort of specifics that can be translated into action, legislative or otherwise.

The one new thing this year is Jacob's idea for financing the completion of the civil rights revolution. He'd pay for it with, say, half of the $300-billion "peace dividend" he reckons will become available as a result of "the end of the Cold War."

"We've been hearing a lot about how there really won't be any [peace dividend]," Jacob told his audience at the National Press Club. "I cannot accept that. Elementary mathematics suggests that when you take $150 billion from $300 billion, you have $150 billion left over. What to do with that $150 billion becomes a test of political wisdom."

Well, there is another test of political wisdom: whether we can learn from recent history that "peace dividends," whether from arms-reductions treaties or the end of the Vietnam War, have a way of disappearing into thin air. Given the administration's commitment to reduce the federal deficit without raising taxes, this latest projected dividend is even likelier than the others to go "poof."

To see why, imagine that you have gone deeply into debt to finance your children's education and that your last child is about to graduate from college. How much time are you going to spend deliberating over what to do with all your extra money?

No, John, there's not going to be any peace dividend—and there needn't be. America will spend what it is convinced it has to spend. Your job is to develop and market specific ideas for meeting the needs you outline so eloquently: not just "education," for instance, but a 10-fold or 20-fold expansion of Head Start; not vague talk about "developing human capital" but specific programs to get the jobless and despairing underclass ready for the employment opportunities demographers are predicting the next decade will bring.

It's true that you can't do these things without money, but it is also true that money is no substitute for intelligent programs. Jacob understands that the reason for the "peace dividend" that has him so hopeful is that both the United States and the Soviet Union have seen the folly of imagining that they could measure national security in dollars and rubles alone. If we are to make an effective claim on this country's constricted resources for the sort of priorities Jacob has in mind, we have to recognize the equal folly of trying to measure progress in combating ignorance, joblessness, adolescent pregnancy and drug abuse primarily in terms of expenditures.

In truth, Jacob's remarks and the 10 major papers presented with them constituted an accurate analysis of the problems that afflict black America: a retrograde Supreme Court, a deteriorating family structure, joblessness, black-on-black crime, poor health and a dearth of affordable housing.

And if Jacob's speech—including his proposal to spend half of the "peace dividend" on domestic social programs—had been given by the president of the United States rather than the president of the Urban League, it would have represented a breakthrough of immense proportions. Imagine President Bush proposing that revolution toward freedom in Eastern Europe be followed by the completion of "*our* unfinished revolution for democracy and human rights," or proclaiming that "the end of the Cold War must mean the start of a renewed drive to bring America into the 21st century by investing in its people and its economy," or calling for "intense national efforts to educate and employ *all* of our people, and to eliminate racism from our national life."

It is enough for the president of the United States to state his priorities, leaving it to his Cabinet and his party's congressional leadership to translate those priorities into programs. The president of the Urban League must assume the additional task of translating his priorities into program proposals that make sense, not just to his constituency but to the majority of the American people.

Maybe John Jacob will do that in the months ahead. He didn't do it yesterday.

(January 1990)

A Plan Black America

Should Adopt

Assemble america's civil rights leaders in a hall and then parade before them 100 black teen-agers.

Bet: Any one of the leaders could look at the youngsters, ask each of them a question calculated to produce a single-sentence reply and then, with startling accuracy, tell you which of them had managed to find a job and which had experienced a run of "bad luck" in his job search. Or which of them was likely to be doing reasonably well in school, or which stood a good chance of winding up solidly middle class.

Question: If these leaders, whose careers are devoted to helping these youngsters, could tell you, virtually at a glance, which of these youngsters was in actual or potential difficulty (and indeed would probably not be hired by the leaders themselves), why the insistence that "the system" is responsible for their plight?

The answer is that the leadership supposes that the alternative is to indict the youngsters themselves: to "blame the victim."

But there is another alternative: We can put the onus on the black leadership—and here I mean not just the heads of organizations but middle-class blacks who constitute the leadership class.

I've just been on the phone with Father George C. Clements of Chicago's Holy Angels Catholic Church, who knows very well what I'm talking about.

Father Clements is the black priest who, back in November, startled his congregation with the announcement that he had made up his mind to adopt a child. Moreover, he said, he would launch a national campaign to urge black families all over America to do the same thing.

He is now awaiting finalization of application to adopt a 12-year-old boy who was abandoned as an infant and has spent most of his life in institutions.

"When I first made the decision, I announced that I wanted a child that nobody else would adopt," he said.

Father Clements is a striking example of practicing what he has been preaching with considerable fervor.

"There are some 2,500 homeless black children in Chicago alone," he said. "I'm told by the Black Child Development Institute that there are something like 100,000 homeless black children in America. That really is a terrible indictment of us, isn't it?

"Bear in mind that what we're talking about is a fairly recent phenomenon. There were hardly any homeless black children before World War II. The reason: the extended-family concept. The community or friends or relatives always took these children in. Nobody thought about demanding that the government do it. We have to get back to the '20s and '30s and get that attitude back. I think it's as important for middle-class blacks as it is for the children themselves."

He said his attitude in this regard was substantially reinforced during a visit last month to Nigeria. "They have no problem with homeless children in Nigeria—again because of the extended-family concept. People here keep telling me that they are strapped financially, that they can't afford to take anyone in, and I tell them that we used to do it, that the Nigerians still do it and their standard of living is far below ours."

Father Clements says he finds it disgraceful that white couples are waiting two, three and four years to adopt, while scores of thousands of black children remain homeless. "How can we let that happen and still talk about black pride and self-respect?"

He places the major burden for changing black middle-class attitudes on the shoulders of the black churches. "We could virtually eliminate the problem if every church would accept the challenge of having at least one member family adopt a child. If the volunteering family had money problems, the entire congregation could join in and help."

The 48-year-old Chicago-born priest notes that adoption isn't the only way that successful black families could contribute to the rescue of the millions of black youngsters who seem destined for the economic junkheap. Almost any contribution would help, he says: tutoring, giving time to children who need time and attention, even giving money to make it possible for others to provide direct help.

The important thing, he said, is for blacks to recognize the problem and to recognize that they must assume a direct role in solving it.

(March 1981)

BUT WHAT ARE THEY FOR?

IF YOU SHARE America's fascination with the emergence of a handful of black conservatives, you know by now what these rare birds are against.

They are against government interference in the free market. They are opposed, quite specifically, to such notions as affirmative action, minimum wage and rent control. They are outraged by licensing requirements for many trades and occupations, opposed to quotas and set-asides for minority entrepreneurs, dismayed by such pro-union legislation as the Davis-Bacon Act.

It is hardly overstating the case to say that they are against virtually all the programs and policies espoused by liberals and civil rights advocates.

Their notions are so unorthodox, at least for blacks, that it's interesting to hear them. It can be fun to talk with a Thomas Sowell about the long-term implications of ending rent control, or to a Walter Williams about the link between black unemployment and the minimum wage laws.

But after a while you are likely to grow weary of hearing what they are *against*. What you'd like to hear them explain, at least in broad outline, is what they are *for*.

I thought we'd get some of those answers when Sowell revealed that he was toying with the idea of forming an alternative civil rights organization, one that would take a conservative approach to black problem-solving. But he recently had a two-part monograph in the *Washington Post* in which he spent nearly all of his considerable space attacking the established black leadership.

He is against their adoption of policies and priorities that are out of step with those of the black masses. He is against the very existence of a black leadership that has no grounding in poverty. He is even against black leadership that is too light of complexion.

But what is he for? What programs and policies would his new organization propose to address the problems confronting black Americans? He didn't tell us.

I have just seen a copy of the *Moral Majority Report*, a 16-page tabloid, that contains among other things two articles by Walter Williams.

One offers a devastating critique of the Davis-Bacon Act, a federal law that requires that workers on federally funded construction jobs be paid the "prevailing" wage, which generally means the union wage. Naturally he calls for repeal of Davis-Bacon.

He also calls for an end to affirmative action programs, set-aside contracts and other such efforts at solving the problems facing black Americans.

I don't intend here to debate the efficacy of those particular approaches. But surely Williams doesn't believe that most black problems result from government efforts to help. Surely he and Sowell will acknowledge that joblessness and poverty existed before the minimum wage, that discrimination didn't begin with affirmative action programs, that low-income blacks had housing problems even before rent control.

And if they acknowledge that much, they must also acknowledge that repeal of those particular efforts won't solve the problems either.

Some of us are wide open to at least *listen* to conservative approaches for solving the problems that the liberal approaches have left unresolved.

But so far we have listened in vain. What we get is the 1980s counterpart of the 1960s rioters whose notion was to tear the system down without any thought of what to put in its place.

Finally you want to shout at them to stop telling you what you've done wrong for all these years and tell you what to do now to solve your problems.

And if they don't know, maybe they should just admit it and go away.

(February 1981)

OUR MISSING ANGER

THE WOMAN LIES NEAR DEATH in a New York hospital, victim not merely of her own foolish daring but also of a singularly bestial attack: vicious, brutish, unprovoked. And I keep wanting the black leadership to say something about it.

Is that silly? What would I want them to say? The 28-year-old woman went jogging in Central Park—*at night*, for heaven's sake—and got in trouble. What's the black leadership got to do with that? What would I want them to say and in what forum?

I suppose I just want them to say that they—that we—are outraged; that we demand justice, that we care about that woman, though she is white and her attackers are black children.

It's easy enough to understand why they aren't talking. To begin with, it isn't one of their issues. Moreover, the attackers are members of their constituency and the victim is not. And finally, they may fear that to speak out as black leaders would spread the guilt from the young savages who did the deed to blacks generally.

After all, it wasn't "black America" that beat, stabbed, gang-raped and battered this hapless woman and left her for dead. It was a group of some 30 children, themselves victims, no doubt, of some social atrocities, who did this savage thing. Why should black leaders buy into the savagery by having anything to say about it one way or another?

And didn't the victim, while not precisely "asking for it," pretty much bring the horror upon herself? She did resist the advice of friends and the common wisdom of New Yorkers: stay the hell out of Central Park at night.

All true. But it is also true that it wasn't "white America" that assaulted the three black men who strayed into Howard Beach, chasing one to his death in the path of a car. It was a mob of white teen-agers.

Still, the black leadership demanded that white leaders speak out about the incident, if only to demonstrate that they weren't all represented by that club-wielding mob. And white leaders did speak out.

As for the notion that the so far unnamed victim of the recent attack should never have gone on a night-time jog in Central Park—no matter how realistic that advice might be—is not very different from saying that those black guys shouldn't have been wandering around in that all-white, blue-collar section of Howard Beach. There shouldn't be places in America where people are forbidden to go because of their race.

I wish the black leadership would say that. I wish we could get over the notion that we have to defend (or at any rate keep silent about) the bad actors among us, even though I understand why we do it.

Sometimes it is simply because they are black and their critics are white; sometimes it is because we fear that for us to turn on even the most blameworthy of blacks would license racists to turn on all of us. As a matter of fact, the opposite is true. But in any case, it is beside the point.

It may also be beside the point that we don't know what to

do about children who, with or without the excuse of poverty, have become such cold-eyed and remorseless monsters. We don't know how to "fix" people who have reached adolescence or adulthood without having internalized any recognizable moral code, and we don't know how to keep from churning out more of them.

But surely our vocal disapproval of their savagery is one place to start.

We need to make it clear that we are outraged by brutality, not just white brutality. We need to find the words to say we care about victims, not just black victims. To keep silent in the face of atrocities committed by blacks erodes the moral value of our outrage when the atrocities are committed by whites.

It is in the interest both of justice and our progress that we espouse common standards against which we can establish sound social policy and hold people accountable for their behavior. And just as Martin Luther King, Jr., found the courage to speak out against the violence of both the Klan and the Black Panthers, it must start with the leadership.

Those race spokesmen, self-appointed and otherwise, who have made it their special mission to attack societal injustice must find the courage to measure that injustice by a single yardstick.

(May 1989)

LITTLE SHORTIES, LITTLE HOPE

THEY CALL THEM, writes *Post* reporter Herbert Denton, "the little shorties."

They are the 11-, 12- and 13-year-olds on the front lines of the brick-throwers and window smashers in Miami's angry Liberty City.

But to see them primarily as teen-age and pre-teen hoodlums is to miss nearly the whole tragedy of their situation, which is that they are hardly dry behind the ears and already almost totally without hope.

Saddest of all, their sense of hopelessness is an accurate reflection of their reality. Look at the world from their point of view and it's almost impossible not to be hopeless.

When you live in poverty and squalor, when the availability of your next meal is genuinely in doubt, when of every 10 black youths you see, eight cannot find work, you cannot dream middle-class dreams of a bright future. You dream, if at all, of survival.

The "little shorties," Denton wrote, have "no hope and, as a result, no fear."

Which is another way of saying that they have weighed their situation and concluded that they have nothing to lose. And so they strike out at "the crackers"—whites who, as they see it, are responsible for their hopelessness.

"You're not talking about a handful of kids," Denton quoted the editor of Miami's black newspaper, the *Miami Courier*, as saying. "You are talking about hundreds, hundreds who have no fear."

The absence of fear is a real concern to the authorities because it removes inhibitions to violence. These children are willing to risk their freedom, even their lives, to lash out at the system that has left them behind. Perhaps from their point of view, they really aren't risking so much.

But if these youngsters aren't afraid, the rest of America ought to be. There is no deadlier threat—to tranquility or to the "system"—than people who reckon that they have nothing to lose, who have no stake in preserving what the rest of us hold dear.

These pitiful and very dangerous souls exist not only in Miami but in slums across America. Their situation (and, consequently, America's) grows worse with each new wave of immigrants who elbow ahead of them for a chance to start at the bottom: Cubans and Haitians in Miami, Mexicans in Texas and California, Vietnamese in cities from Arlington to Des Moines.

The rationale for preferring the new immigrants to home-grown blacks is that the former are ambitious and the latter don't really want to work. (People keep on uttering this slander even when, in Miami, blacks find themselves suddenly ineligible for the low-grade jobs that used to be available because they now require fluency in Spanish.)

As a matter of fact, the most hopeful finding in Denton's dismal report is that the "little shorties" want desperately to work, although it's anybody's guess how long this last remnant of humanness will last.

Before it's too late, America must be made to recognize that the story of Liberty City is no more than an exaggeration of the story of the U.S. slums and to start looking for ways not to prevent the occasional explosion of despair but to solve the problem of uselessness.

The common characteristic of the most explosive slums, from Miami's Liberty City to Los Angeles' Watts, is the disappearance of business enterprise. While our leaders are busy fighting inflation, they might more usefully look for ways to entice businesses—black-owned businesses, preferably, but businesses of some kind—into the bombed-out central cities.

Business activity would help to halt the spreading blight, and the revenues would make it possible to provide vital services to this frustrated underclass.

But the real bottom line would be the creation of jobs and the sense of hope that comes from being productive.

"Little shorties" do grow up.

(August 1980)

A PATERNITY SUIT

WITH A DIFFERENCE

IT'S ONE OF THOSE wouldn't-it-be-wonderful-if stories, and it would have made a lovely Father's Day column if I had come across it in time. A young man has asked the court to declare that he *is* the father of a boy born three years ago to an unwed mother. And it's not just any young man who filed the unorthodox paternity suit. It is LeVar Burton, the 26-year-old actor who played the young Kunta Kinte in the TV series "Roots."

Burton said he hadn't even known of the child's existence. But, according to his attorney, Gloria Allred, "after tests confirmed the child was, in fact, his, he decided to do everything possible to assume equal responsibility for his son." He asked the Los Angeles Superior Court to grant him joint legal custody and visitation rights. He also volunteered to pay $600 a month child support. "I grew up in a broken home, raised by my mother," he explained. "I would like for [my son] to have the benefits of both parents."

Wouldn't it be wonderful if more fathers took seriously their responsibilities toward their children, including those born out of wedlock? Wouldn't it be wonderful if we could come to grips with the fact that for every unwed mother who must do what she can to rear her offspring there is an unwed father for whom the enterprise is more or less optional?

Scores of recent studies agree that the children most at risk—economically, socially, educationally—are children of single parents. Single-parent families are the fastest-growing poverty group in America, and the disproportionate contributor to this pool of poverty is the father-absent black family. There are a lot of reasons this is so, among them the fact that low-income black males find it harder than their female counterparts to get work; the fact that oppression is particularly erosive of the qualities we regard as "manly"; the fact that marriage and family no longer are the central values they used to be in America.

But one reason, too, is that, for some of us at least, taking care of a family is no longer a major part of being a man. Our cities are full of young (and not-so-young) men who are proud to have proven their manhood by getting their girlfriends pregnant. They go around with their chests poked out when they might more appropriately hang their heads in shame.

Wouldn't it be wonderful if reaching out to take care of out-of-wedlock children became the "macho" thing to do? Wouldn't it be wonderful if the ascription of manliness that used to come from merely siring children were withheld from men who fail to take care of their children to the best of their ability?

The thing about LeVar Burton is that he understands that manhood isn't about making babies. He said he didn't know that his one-night encounter with a young woman he hardly knew had produced a baby until the district attorney told him. But once he found out, he moved quickly to meet his parental responsibility. Wouldn't it be wonderful if LeVar Burton's became the accepted definition of what it is to be a man?

(June 1988)

WHAT CAN BE DONE?

THE HOWARD UNIVERSITY PROFESSOR was on the phone because he "just had to talk to somebody." He is dismayed and frightened, he said, over the plight of the black underclass and frustrated that middle-class black professionals don't seem interested in doing anything about it.

"It's increasingly obvious that the federal government isn't going to do anything about the problem—I'm not sure how much it could do if it wanted to—and that it's up to the black middle class to do something about it. But when you talk to your friends about it, you get statements like: 'The best thing I can do for the underclass is to be the best doctor I can be, to set an example of success.' That's a cop-out. The problem is getting worse all the time, and something has to be done."

The engineer friend who called me at home a few hours later apologized for bending my ear, but he "just had to talk" about the problem. He had lunched at a small soul-food restaurant near his place of business and was shocked at the language—loud, unrestrained and obscene—of three black adolescents who had come into the place. "I'm no prude; my friends and I used some of the same language when I was growing up. The difference is, we would never have said such things in the presence of adults.

"You'd like to think of trying to help some of these kids find a job, or possibly hiring some of them. But the truth is, I'm afraid of them. These kids are going to be lost unless we figure out some way of rescuing them. But what?"

Which, of course, is the problem. Those of us who were the beneficiaries of the earlier civil-rights movement—whose middle-class attitudes of academic preparation and hard work enabled us to take advantage of the opportunities that movement made available—have not been able to devise a comparable breakthrough for the growing underclass.

The youngsters most in need of help seem least ready for it. They lack the basic skills and, more dismayingly, the basic attitudes that would make them attractive even as entry-level employees. They don't know how to seek the help they need, and worse, they positively frighten those who feel the urge to offer help.

We are helpless, idea-less witnesses to a near-total social breakdown. The concerned professionals who could command the resources don't know what to do. Members of the youngsters' own families, who at an earlier time might have helped them learn the attitudes that would help them secure the special help they need, often don't have the appropriate attitudes themselves, having spent most of their lives outside the formal job structure. In a growing number of instances, their households hardly qualify as families at all.

Can anything be done? I suspect that there may be a fair number of middle-class blacks who, like the Howard University professor and the engineer, would be ready to help if there was some mechanism for doing so. One such mechanism might be a formal organization, locally based, for pairing these disaster-bound youngsters with middle-class adults who could help them develop the academic and attitudinal basis for escaping the underclass: a sort of Big Brothers approach designed to inculcate middle-class values.

But Big Brothers itself has a huge backlog of unmatched youngsters, due to the desperate shortage of volunteering black men. Still, I believe a properly established organization, with a well-run publicity and recruitment campaign, could produce worthwhile results.

There would still be a shortage of role models, the demographics being what they are, but it should be possible to start a "skimming" process in which at least those youngsters (and their parents) who are most interested might get the help they need in breaking out of the desperate pathology of the ghetto.

The alternative is too horrible to contemplate.

(May 1985)

BLACK HELP FOR BLACK MALES

IT IS BY NOW a commonplace to speak of black men as an "endangered species." What is less common is to move from *de*scription to *pre*scription.

That is the chief reason why what could have been a gloom-and-doom document—a task force report, commissioned by the Montgomery County NAACP, on the declining college participation of black men—is so encouraging.

There is plenty of gloom in the report issued last Saturday. Between 1976 and 1988, the incidence of males among black college graduates fell from 46 percent to 35 percent. Black men are less likely than either white men or black women to enter college and more likely to drop out before graduation. And the implications are deadly. Not only does curtailed education reduce the employability and earning power of black men, but it also makes them less eligible as husbands for better educated black women and impoverishes black families.

The task force might have satisfied itself with an indictment of the general society. After all, blacks in Maryland, though their need is greater, receive fewer and smaller college scholarships than whites. But the focus of the report, based on a 14-month study of state and national trends, is less interested in assigning blame than in fashioning solutions.

Its three dozen recommendations for recapturing "the underutilized population" of black men are aimed at state officials, business leaders and the education system, but also at the black community—including black men themselves.

For instance, it challenges colleges to increase their efforts to recruit and keep black males, businesses and the state to provide more scholarship help, community colleges to work harder at encouraging black males to transfer to four-year institutions and public schools to do a better job of getting black male students ready for college work.

But it also calls on fraternities, churches and social groups to work with young black men to persuade them of the importance of college training. And it calls on black students, particularly males, "to understand the empowerment which higher education provides" and "to excel and refuse to accept failure as an alternative."

As Roscoe Nix, president of the county NAACP branch, put it:

"There is a long tradition of self-help in the black community. It is one thing to lament and agonize and wring our hands. The least we can do is try to start somewhere, regardless of how small."

There is no dearth of places to start. It would be extremely useful, for instance, to know why college-age black men are more than twice as likely as their white counterparts to choose military service over college, or why black students, who are twice as likely to need scholarship help, get less of it than whites.

But it would also be worth the effort to try to change the academic attitudes of black children, particularly black boys. For instance, it would be useful to chart the academic progress of black children to see where—and why—the school attitudes of boys and girls start to diverge and then invite, beg, cajole and embarrass successful blacks (particularly black men) into signing on as advisers, mentors and role models.

Black collegians and professionals—and not just blacks, for that matter—might put aside their fraternity/sorority rivalries to enroll in Delta Sigma Theta Sorority's "School America" campaign to enroll a million "registered readers" to read aloud to at least one child once a week for the balance of the year. Who knows how inspiring it might be for busy adults to show our children that they care about their education.

Too many black children, boys and girls, fail to grasp the implications of undereducation, for themselves and for black America's future. But, as the NAACP report stresses, the problem is so acute among black males as to constitute a crisis.

There is much that the general society can do, and the report, while remarkably free of accusation, offers a number of specific suggestions.

But there is also plenty for the black community itself to do. And perhaps its most important task is to excise the deadly notion that academic exertion is unmasculine and unblack, and (which may be the same thing) to convince black youngsters that they are as smart as anyone else and that they can achieve if they work at it.

As John W. Diggs, chairman of the 15-member task force put it, most of the effort "will have to come from the black community.

"Any people who leave the education of its people to another people is a doomed people."

(January 1990)

RESCUE THE CHILDREN

OF THE UNDERCLASS

THREE RINGING CHEERS for the decision taken over the weekend to form a National Association of Black Organizations to mount a unified attack on the problems besetting black America.

As the NAACP said in calling the meeting of some 100 civic, social and civil rights groups, it is time to "take control of our own destiny... [and] attack the problems afflicting our community with the best weapon at our disposal—black unity."

But the truth is that forming the coalition was the easy step. The difficult part will be deciding what to do: establishing priorities and the techniques for achieving them.

There is no dearth of possibilities: civil rights legislation, full-employment legislation, joint self-help undertakings to enhance academic achievement, an assault on the "glass ceiling" that thwarts the progress of black executives, black economic development, anti-drug efforts, political empowerment, moral renascence. All these things are deserving of attention.

But since any attempt to do everything at once is likely to

mean that nothing gets done all that well, it makes sense to decide on one or two priority goals, at least for the next few years. What should they be?

A nine-member executive committee of the coalition will meet shortly to work out details. I wouldn't want to preempt the committee's deliberations, but I hope the members will pay some attention to what strikes me as a worthy top priority: rescuing the children of the underclass.

It seems clear to me that whatever the problems of black Americans generally, the problems of the inner city constitute a special case. And so many of those problems stem from the pessimism with which inner-city children view their future.

They drop out of school, or get through school with minimal academic effort, because they don't believe that academic exertion will make much difference in their lives. They become adolescent parents because they see no good reason for postponing, or even being particularly careful with, sexual activity. They sell drugs because the money is attractive and the risk of a police record seems small when measured against their chances of success in the legitimate world.

The boys especially are victims of this all-encompassing pessimism. They are unwanted, and often feared, by employers. The resultant joblessness means that they are economically useless (or worse) both to their families and as husbands to the mothers of their own children. And these children, especially the boys, grow up fatherless, never learning what it means to be a responsible husband and father, which means they are overwhelmingly likely to repeat the cycle of uselessness.

Whatever else the National Association of Black Organizations does, it ought to commit itself—commit *us*—to rescuing these luckless children.

And how might we do that? One place to begin would be to undertake a massive Big Brother/Big Sisters-style effort to match inner-city children with mentors, role models and guides from the black middle class. These adult counselors could, by their influence, their personal guidance and their own example, help our discouraged youngsters to see that they have it within their power to break the chains of poverty and despair.

They could also be of enormous assistance in helping them to find jobs, job-training opportunities and scholarships, and in persuading the larger society to make more opportunities available. But their greatest contribution might be in helping the youngsters to understand and abandon the attitudes that limit their life chances.

It would also be well for us to understand—and counter— the rewards that accrue to inner-city youngsters for their deadly behavior: not just the money from crack sales and other unlawful activity, but the admiration of their peers. We need to find ways to offer status and other more tangible rewards to youngsters who behave as we think they ought to behave.

Instead of providing the most help for those children most in need of help, it might make sense to offer the most help to those for whom that help could make a permanent difference. I have referred to it as "skimming": identifying the young people who "present" themselves as exemplars of the behavior we urge and then giving them rewards consonant with their good behavior.

The behavior could be anything from perfect school atten- dance and good grades to volunteer work, good citizenship and general academic and social improvement; the rewards could range from status-symbol sneakers and spending cash to guarantees of scholarships and career-oriented jobs. The point is that the rewards must confer status within the children's own environment.

Obviously there are other worthwhile targets, including the academic underperformance of the children of the middle class, the economic underdevelopment of the black community and, yes, racism.

But the biggest problem in black America—perhaps the biggest social and economic threat to the entire country—is the plight of the children in the inner cities. It's time to mount a full-scale crusade to rescue them.

(August 1990)

COSBY SHOW: BLACK OR WHITE?

"THE QUESTION IS BEING ASKED more and more by reporters," says the black Harvard professor, arguably America's best-known psychiatrist. "Its purpose is not clear, but it seems to be framed as an attack, calculated to make us feel guilty."

"The question" has nothing to do with Reagan's likely reelection, or cuts in social programs, or the future of Jesse Jackson. The question Alvin Poussaint has grown tired of hearing is this: "Is the 'Bill Cosby Show' black or white?"

The Bill Cosby show, for those who spend all their TV time watching Ted Koppel or "The Six Wives of Henry VIII," is the season's hottest new family sitcom: ingratiating, well-acted and funny. But the "Huxtables" (Cosby's TV family) are not public housing residents or recent escapees from the ghetto or wise-cracking domestics or overweight nannies. Their children don't spend their time running con games or explaining their innocence to the authorities.

He is a physician; she is a lawyer; the kids are pretty much like yours, though cuter. And the question keeps coming: is the family black enough?

Poussaint, who gets the calls because he has been retained to review the show's scripts for psychological consistency, racial authenticity and freedom from unintended insult, admits a degree of bafflement. He was especially baffled, he says, by a reviewer in the *Village Voice* who described the "Huxtables" as "quite determinedly [not] black in anything but their skin color. I don't mean just in their lifestyle—even their cultural background, and their whole context of reference, is that of American Caucasians." Then: "Some white liberals and the few blacks who care may think of Cosby as a sellout, but the truth is that he...no longer qualifies as black enough to be an Uncle Tom."

Other critics have settled for milder putdowns: "'Father Knows Best' in blackface," (*Newsweek*) or "racial neuter."

Very few of the criticisms come from black viewers, Poussaint says. "I'm not sure what the white reporters are complaining of," he said in a recent interview. "Sometimes it seems they want the show to be 'culturally' black in the sense that they think of cultural blackness—like the Jeffersons or 'Good Times'— and sometimes it seems they would be happier to see them cussing out white people, a sort of protest sitcom. Some seem to feel that because the family is middle-class with no obvious racial problems, that constitutes a denial or dismissal of the black poor. And some seem to feel somehow threatened."

Far be it from me to invade the psychiatrist's turf, but it may be that many whites really do doubt that a solidly middle-class black family can be as authentic as a solidly middle-class white family. Maybe they really don't know that there are growing numbers of black families whose life styles are a lot closer to the "Huxtables" than to the "Jeffersons," that you don't have to be poverty-stricken or bitter or smart-ass to be authentic.

No doubt these well-off black families spend more time talking about racial matters than do the "Huxtables" but so, I suspect, do the real-life counterparts of the folk on "Cheers."

Some politically sensitive viewers might prefer that the

Cosby clan take advantage of the opportunity to educate its huge audience on the nuances of racism. But carefully. There is the danger that too much "message" could destroy a show whose survival depends on being funny.

Besides, there is value in letting white America understand that blackness isn't necessarily a pathological condition.

(November 1984)

EMBARRASSING QUESTIONS

A MAN I KNOW was driving his 11-year-old son home the other night when the youngster hit him with a question from out of the blue.

"Daddy," he wondered, "do white people take drugs?"

Of course they do, my friend answered.

"Well," said the boy, "I never hear anything about it."

My friend didn't know what to make of that brief conversation. I don't either, but I'm afraid it stands as an indictment of the calling in which I earn my living: journalism.

How could a bright young black child with the economic and intellectual advantages of a middle-class family reach the conclusion that drug abuse is the result of some peculiar character flaw of black people? The answer is that our reporting virtually forces the conclusion.

We know that the drug-ridden inner-city neighborhoods represent only the public manifestation of a problem that permeates the society. We are aware of the statistics indicating that perhaps 70 to 80 percent of the consumption of illicit drugs happens outside the ghettos. We know that poor people haven't enough money to sustain the international trafficking in drugs or to turn it into an obscenely lucrative business. But that knowledge rarely informs our stories and commentaries. Why?

I think there are two main reasons. The first is that white and middle-class drug abusers are far less likely than their inner-city counterparts to come to the attention of the police and therefore to the attention of the media. Their drug deals and their drug consumption are more likely to take place in private, with minimal risk of arrest. There are few open-air drug markets in the white parts of town, few trials of white drug kingpins (or money launderers or importers of illegal narcotics), few beeper-equipped white kids walking the halls of our high schools. The public problem of drugs is overwhelmingly an inner-city problem.

The second reason—the reason I have contributed to the false impression of my friend's son—is that it is black neighborhoods that are by far the most likely to be overwhelmed by drugs. I write about drugs in the inner cities because that is where we find the drug violence, the murders, the wrecked communities, crack babies and other manifestations of the appalling effects of the deadly traffic in drugs.

White people, though they may suffer the horror of drug abuse, tend to suffer as individuals, and in private. Blacks suffer as entire communities, no matter that the overwhelming majority in the most depressed ghettos never become involved with drugs.

But if that explains my frequent focus on drug abuse among blacks, I'm still dismayed by my contribution to the misperceptions of that 11-year-old boy—and, no doubt, thousands like him. Indeed it occurs to me that he might have asked a whole series of embarrassing questions based on what he learns from me and my fellow journalists.

Daddy, do people in the inner cities ever do anything worthwhile? Do they love their children, care about their education, fear for their future, encourage their ambition? Daddy, are all tutors and other volunteers white? Are there no superlative teachers in the schools in low-income neighborhoods? Daddy, are there any white people on welfare? In jail? Guilty of abuse of office? Having children out of wedlock or as teenage parents?

Daddy, what's *wrong* with us?

I know that many of the social problems that occupy us are problems that are likely to be exacerbated by poverty and despair and that blacks are the disproportionate victims of both poverty and despair. But the youngster's question—and the questions he might have asked—should prompt us, both as parents and as journalists, to emphasize the connection of these problems to poverty rather than to race. His innocent inquiry should lead us to a more balanced investigation and discussion of what we already know.

For instance, the No. 1 cash crop of both Kentucky and California is marijuana. Do we believe that producers and customers for these illicit crops are mostly inner-city blacks? Do we believe that the bankers and other businessmen who launder the proceeds of the traffic in narcotics are residents of the black ghettos? Do we believe that the billions of dollars made in the deadly traffic in cocaine and heroin are enriching the black community?

We know better, but you couldn't tell it from our news accounts. Don't we owe it to that 11-year-old—and to all our children—to provide a more complete context in which they can think about the problems that beset the American society?

Daddy, what's wrong with the media?

(August 1990)

SYMPATHY FOR THOSE LIKE US

SUNDAY'S FRONT-PAGE STORY was an account of a 27-year-old Capitol Hill aide who had been arrested on a drug charge. I found the story disturbing. Not disturbing as in annoying, but disturbing as in unsettling, as in breaking up the serenity of, as in thought-provoking.

What disturbed me—and apparently a fair number of other readers—was the sympathetic treatment of the young man.

He was described, not as a junkie charged with making a heroin buy from an undercover cop, but as a "golden youth" whose life has been permanently tarnished. The son of a survivor of the Holocaust, he had graduated magna cum laude from Harvard, where he also earned his law degree. He had nearly completed work on his doctorate (London School of Economics) and was earning some $40,000 a year as a member of the staff of Pat Moynihan's Senate Select Committee on Intelligence.

The burden of the story, replete with glowing praise from

well-placed friends, was grief over a brilliant career turned suddenly, perhaps irrevocably, sour.

And all I could think of was how fortunate he was to receive such sympathetic treatment in the hard-nosed press. I thought of the hundreds of stories of drug arrests we have had over the years, and how little sympathy those stories reflected for the arrestees. Why was this one handled differently?

The ostensible reason is the lost promise of this brilliant young man, who might have contributed so much to society. And yet, I wonder what sort of social good we expected from this neo-conservative young scholar on a Senate Intelligence Committee. Moreover, he wasn't alone at the time of his arrest, but in the company of "another lawyer," who was not further described in the story. Didn't the arrest of that lawyer (who subsequently took an overdose of Valium) also represent lost promise?

What happened, I suspect, is that reporter Ronald Kessler, like a lot of *Post* readers who saw his piece, can identify with 27-year-old Eric Breindel. If he had chosen journalism rather than the law and economics, he might well have worked in the *Post* newsroom. Breindel's was one of those but-for-the-grace-of-God stories that can evoke the sympathy of the similarly situated. My guess is that few low-income blacks read that story and came away saddened over lost potential. In fact, I've talked to a fair number of middle-class blacks who wonder what all the hoopla was about.

On the other hand, some of these same middle-class blacks were saddened when the clean-cut, middle-class John Lucas let drugs destroy a professional basketball career. If there was no such black middle-class sympathy for Marvin "Bad News" Barnes, another pro basketballer, it was because the middle-class blacks could see Lucas, but not Barnes, as a case of but-for-the-grace-of-God.

In other words, it's not about race but about the ability of reporters to identify. Nor is my point that Kessler's piece was unduly sympathetic. He didn't try to paint Breindel (whose resignation Moynihan demanded after the arrest) as an innocent, but only as a human being—something reporters have trouble doing for people who are very different from themselves. What Kessler's story makes clear for me is the value of making newsroom staffs as broadly representative as possible: racially, economically and otherwise. A lot of the people we write about, not just the brilliant ones who find themselves in predicaments, could be written about with a little more human understanding and sympathy—not to help them escape the penalties of their mistakes but to help our readers understand something of the pressures and frailties that lead some of us to do stupid things.

(May 1983)

NAMES THAT HURT

IF JAMES WATT HAD DESCRIBED his coal-leasing commission as comprising "a woman, a black, two Jews and a handicapped person," he'd still be secretary of the interior. It was his use of the word "cripple" that tagged him as insensitive and cost him his job.

Which raises a question that's been bothering me: Why is "cripple" an insensitive thing to say? Part of the answer, of course, is that it can be demeaning to be treated as a nominalized adjective. "She is a black woman" sounds less offensive than "She is a black"; "He has epilepsy" is less harsh than "He is an epileptic," and "He is crippled" is better than "He is a cripple."

But that isn't all of it. The word "crippled," notwithstanding the esteem in which the Crippled Children's Society used to be held, has been out of favor for some time, having been replaced by "handicapped."

Before you start thinking that you understand why, ask yourself why, in more recent times, "handicapped" itself has fallen into disfavor. The acceptable designation these days is "disabled," as in the International Year of the Disabled.

Logic would suggest that, at least when it comes to employment opportunity, those who suffer from one impairment or another would prefer to be called "handicapped," which has a sporting ring to it, rather than "disabled," which seems to call attention to what they cannot do. Obviously, logic has little to do with it. What does?

Evan Kemp, who has spent a lot of years thinking about such things, offers the notion that the "acceptable" designations for a particular out-of-favor group keep changing every generation or so until that group is integrated into society. Whatever name is in vogue at the point of social acceptance will be the lasting one.

"As long as a group is ostracized or otherwise demeaned, whatever name is used to designate that group will eventually take on a demeaning flavor and have to be replaced," he says. Thus "idiot," which used to be the term of choice, has long since given way to "exceptional," and "deaf" and "blind" are being superseded by "hearing-impaired" and "sight-impaired," just as "crippled" has given way to "handicapped," which is giving way to "disabled," which, unless society changes its attitude, will give way to something else.

"Black" is sticking as the acceptable designation for Afro-Americans, he said, because that's what they called themselves in the 1960s when they came to be accepted as a legitimate part of the culture.

Kemp, who teaches disability law at Catholic University, works for the Disability Rights Center in Washington and is part-owner of a wheelchair manufacturing company, says he often finds himself getting "sharp" with people inside the disability-rights movement who object too strenuously to the use of the word "handicapped." (He uses "handicapped" and "disabled" interchangeably.)

Right now, he said, he's resisting pressure to change the name of the wheelchair company from Invacare to something that does not evoke "invalid," another disfavored designation.

Indeed "wheelchair" is in disfavor, though no one has come up with a good substitute word.

Kemp isn't looking. He understands that the problem isn't words but attitudes: attitudes like those he confronted two decades ago when he graduated at the top of his University of Virginia law class, booked himself into 39 interviews with law firms and racked up 39 flat refusals. The reason, he says, is the wheelchair to which he has been confined since childhood as the result of a polio-like illness.

That rude introduction to the "real world," he says, is what led him to his commitment to disability rights—not to change the names by which the physically impaired are designated but to "change the public attitude toward people who are different."

(November 1983)

WHEN BLACK BECOMES

AFRICAN AMERICAN

THE QUESTION (though I must have been out of the room when it was asked) is what to call people who look like me. The answer (though I seem to have missed the meeting at which it was debated and decided) is African American.

No problem. I can learn to call myself—to think of myself as—African American as easily as I learned to call myself colored, Negro and black. It's just that I was unaware, until the Rev. Jesse Jackson told me a couple of weeks ago, that the African American masses out there were seething with indignation, ready to stand up and demand that they be called by their right name. (Sixty-two percent of the respondents to a call-in survey taken by the *Chicago Sun-Times* said they preferred "African American" to "black.")

The recommended term, say Jackson and a small group of co-ethnic leaders, is a way of affirming a heritage that predates our arrival here as slaves, a way of ameliorating our cultural identity crisis. In addition, it is more consistent with other ethnic designations.

"To be called African American has cultural integrity," Jackson has said. "Just as you have Chinese Americans who have a sense of roots in China, or Europeans, every ethnic group in the country has a reference to some land base, some historical, cultural base."

It's true, and I'm perfectly willing to be an African American, though I confess that I was happy enough with black. Except for one thing.

It has long bothered me that in lists of ethnic minorities, black is the only one that (in most American newspapers) is spelled in lower case, as in: "The survey included Hispanics, Asian Americans, American Indians and blacks."

A fair number of people I know believe the lower-casing of "black" is a deliberate racial put-down. The truth, of course, is that until the emergence of the "black pride" movement of the 1960s, we were Negroes, nicely capitalized, while "white" was spelled with a small "w." When newspapers, at our insistence, made the shift from Negro to black, we lost the capitalization in favor of consistency. Not Black and white, but black and white. A style change to Black and White would solve my problem.

But not that of Jackson and the others, who see a change to "African American" as a sort of cultural coming of age.

It's not a universal sentiment, even among those to whom the designation would apply. For instance, Charles Wright, founder and chairman of the board of Detroit's Museum of African American History, thinks the fledgling campaign constitutes a dissipation of energies that could better be applied to addressing such problems as leaving school, drug abuse and slaughter of black men.

"We could concentrate on those three, and we'd have our hands full," he told Reuter.

"We have kids that are going to be really out of step with the technological developments in the country. They are not only unemployed but unemployable, and we should be doing something about that right now instead of worrying about what Jesse Jackson says."

The more interesting question, though, is why, after learning to embrace "black" and forcing it into the white vocabulary (after years of "black" as racial insult), is there this incipient effort to change the designation once again.

The best answer may have been supplied five years ago by Evan Kemp of the Washington-based Disability Rights Center. I had asked Kemp to explain the shift from "crippled" to "handicapped" to "disabled" to describe the people on whose behalf he worked. In particular, I asked, why the abandonment of "handicapped," which, to my mind, had a sporting ring to it, in favor of "disabled," which seems to call attention to what they cannot do? His answer:

"As long as a group is ostracized or otherwise demeaned, whatever name is used to designate that group will eventually take on a demeaning flavor and have to be replaced. The designation will keep changing every generation or so until the group is integrated into society. Whatever name is in vogue at the point of social acceptance will be the lasting one."

If Kemp is right, and I don't doubt it, the campaign to install "African American" as the preferred term for descendants of slaves—no matter how compelling the argument for it—may be a reflection less of logic than of despair.

After a quarter-century of optimism regarding our eventual acceptance into the American mainstream, we sense a turning back of the racial clock: in white impatience with black complaints of injustice, in the increased bigotry on college campuses, in the treatment of presidential candidate Jackson, even in the media assaults on Washington Mayor Marion Barry.

That renewed sense of our outsideness may be the real force behind the drive to change the name by which we are called.

(January 1989)

WHY THE RACIAL SLOGANS?

"IT'S A BLACK THING. You Wouldn't Understand."

I've been seeing the slogan on buttons, badges and shirts—including one in my own home—for some time now. At first it struck me as clever and no more offensive than the "Black Is Beautiful" slogan of 20 years ago.

Maybe it still is. But I've been trying various versions of the sentiment and trying to figure out why some versions seem benign, some hostile and some merely sort of goofy.

A black student wearing the "Black Thing" (or "Black Thang," as it sometimes appears) slogan on a Georgetown street would be seen as hip, humorous and race-conscious in a healthy sort of way.

At least I *think* that's how he would be seen. The slogan would seem (to me) to say nothing more hostile than, "We have our own expressions, our own ways of dealing among ourselves. I could explain Rasti locks or the latest slang, but, hey, what's the point? You've got your symbols, we've got ours."

But show me a white student with a "It's a White Thing..."
sweat shirt, and my attitude changes. What do you mean I
wouldn't understand? Are you saying I'm ignorant or stupid or
culturally deprived?

"It's a (blank) Thing; You Wouldn't Understand."

Fill in the blank with, say, "Women's," and I see, at worst, a
reasonably liberated woman making a slight dig at men. Insert
"Harvard," and I see an immature intellectual snob.

"It's a Male Thing..." "It's an Irish Thing..." "It's a Jewish
Thing..." "It's a WASP Thing..." "It's a Chicano Thing..."
Do they all rate the same on the benign/hostile scale?

And if they don't, why don't they?

My own reactions (certainly no infallible guide) vary with
the social status of the group touting its specialness. I see
low-prestige outgroups—gays, Chicanos, blacks, Towson State—
as saying: No matter what you think, I feel good about myself.
High-prestige groups, on the other hand, appear to be rub-
bing it in.

Examples abound. "My Other Car Is a Rolls Royce," displayed on the bumper sticker of a VW beetle, is a joke. The
same bumper sticker on a new Buick may be dismissed as
wishful thinking. On a Bentley, it is apt to be taken literally
and, therefore, becomes insufferable boasting.

Students at Howard University would almost certainly re-
sent it if American University's radio station advertised itself as
broadcasting "360 degrees of whiteness." And yet, before it
grew up to become a major player among the city's broadcast
outlets, Howard's radio station saw nothing offensive about
claiming "360 degrees of blackness."

Maybe growing up—in status if not in maturity—is a part of
it. You cannot claim both full equality and special dispensation.

Publicly displayed group-consciousness may be an admirable
attempt to transform negative perceptions into positive ones.
But it also amounts to an acknowledgment of inferior status.

The Congressional Black Caucus is legitimate only because
it exists as an acknowledgment that blacks still have a lot of
catching up to do. A Congressional White Caucus is unthink-

able. The National Association for the Advancement of Colored People is a revered civil rights organization. Not so the late, unlamented National Association for the Advancement of White People. "White Is Beautiful" is the slogan of bigots.

The telling clue is whether nonmembers of the group view your publicly asserted pride as benign or hostile.

That's why I don't insist that young blacks get rid of their "It's a Black Thing..." buttons, badges and sweat shirts.

Once they really start to feel equal and expect the world to treat them as equals, they will feel less need for the race-conscious slogans. "Black Is Beautiful" was legitimate in the days when white America thought it wasn't. With the crowning of the third black Miss America, it is a redundancy.

People who feel superior wouldn't dream of advertising the fact. Superior people know it's rude to rub it in.

(September 1989)

LOOKING BACKWARD AT US

IN THE HEAT OF OUR DEBATES over so many issues that trouble us, it's a little hard to accept that our grandchildren will find most of our arguments silly.

It is hard enough to accept when the issues are scientific: whether to move forward with nuclear power development, for instance. It's a good deal harder, and more than slightly humbling, when the issues are over morality: right and wrong.

I'm not predicting how the debates will be resolved, only that they will be resolved, and so conclusively that it will seem weird to future generations that the debates ever took place.

Take the question of abortion. Maybe my grandchildren will find it laughable that so many of us even dreamed of questioning the right of a woman to decide whether to carry a pregnancy to term—just as it strikes us as silly that our grandparents took seriously the question of whether it should be legal to buy a bottle of liquor.

Or maybe they will be aghast that people in Grandpop's day

spent time debating whether a fetus was something other than a human being—just as we are aghast that an earlier generation spent time debating the humanity of black slaves.

One way or another, the answer will be clear. Or, perhaps more likely, the question itself will have evaporated. Surely science will learn to discover the fact of pregnancy in its first days, or even hours. And surely it will learn to fashion substitutes for the human womb as an incubator for bringing these brand-new fetuses to term. And when that happens, all our talk of trimesters and fetal viability will seem hopelessly silly.

Similarly with today's other burning moral questions, including what to do about the hopelessly ill and, especially, seriously deformed infants.

That last question is hot right now in England, where a pediatrician has just been acquitted of attempted murder for ordering the withholding of medical care from a Mongoloid baby. A recent poll of British pediatricians found more than 59 percent of them in favor of allowing severely handicapped babies who are rejected by their parents to die. In the case of babies with spina bifida (open spine), the number of doctors saying they would withhold treatment reached 70 percent.

The question is very difficult for us because we see it as inextricably bound up with the questions of eugenics and euthanasia. If we let babies die because they are grotesquely abnormal, won't we also be tempted to withhold medical treatment from babies who are physically or mentally less than perfect? And if we allow hopelessly ill adults to decide against medical efforts to save them, won't the next step be to make a similar decision on behalf of those who are too ill to make it for themselves? These are, for us, deeply troubling moral questions.

But 100 years from now, the questions are likely to be so easy as to be hardly worth talking about. They will have been resolved by consensus.

Even the notion of morality-by-consensus will strike a lot of us as immoral. We like to think that things are right or wrong regardless of the popular attitude. Our grandchildren are likely to understand that morality-by-consensus is the only societal morality there is. Individuals may opt out of the consensus, just as some individuals reject such commonly accepted medical procedures as blood transfusions. But when most people accept a thing as right or wrong, that is the end of the moral debate.

"My liberal friends in the ACLU would have jumped all over the Dred Scott decision, which held that a slave was less than a human being," one pro-life liberal told me. "Well, it is my opinion that one day we'll look back at *Roe v. Wade* [the 1973 Supreme Court ruling upholding the legality of abortion] as our Dred Scott decision."

Maybe. It may be just as likely that our grandchildren will see a woman's right to an abortion as no more arguable than, say, women's suffrage. The only certainty is that they won't share our confusion.

Sometimes I think it would be nice if we could learn to look at our present-day contentions from the viewpoint of future generations and save ourselves the necessity of moral anguish.

Unfortunately, the questions—and the agonizing—won't be postponed. We have to do our moral wrestling now.

It just might reduce the level of our moral arrogance, though, if we understood that, 100 years from now, our best-crafted arguments will strike another generation as the 1980s version of angels and pinheads.

(November 1981)